So
You Think
You Know It All
Huh...?
(Life's "Short" Journey)

******

By
Antonio Salacuri

"So You Think You Know It All"
Huh...?
(Life's "Short" Journey)
By
Antonio Salacuri

All rights reserved
No part of this publication may be reproduced in any material form; Including photocopying or storing it in any medium by electronic means without the written permission of the copyright owner

Warning:
This book is what they call... Brilliant read...!!!
For that reason and that reason alone you mite be temped to do something... you know what
Please allow me to remind you that;
The doing of an unauthorized act in relation to a copyright work may result in both, civil claim for damages AND most certainly a criminal prosecution
To put it mildly;
"Don't even think about it"
Thank you kindly for understanding

ISBN
978-0-9558556-3-4

So
You Think
You Know It All
Huh...?
(Life's "short" Journey)

Prologos

Hi there;
I am Antonio Salacuri, yes, the author of this "brilliant read" and that quote was made by a number of readers AND a few critiques around the world;
This book is all about what a man would or rather could or maybe even should expect to go through his entire life and I mean from the day he comes into this world;
From that day on is described in so many words, near enough what one will go through every stage of one's life as he grows up;
Every stage as a grown up;
Every stage as a married man;
Every stage as a father as well as a husband;
What responsibilities lie ahead;
What to accept and what not to;
When one should "give in" and when not to;

What to expect once married;
What to expect when... a father;
What to expect from life in general;
What to expect when old-ish and grey;
What to accept and what not to;
Who one's best friend is and who we think it is;
In this book there's everything one needs to know about life in general from day one to near enough... the end of one's life;
But; also in this book one would read how it is possible to get free education or at least I, and I mean me as an author try to "inspire" the younger generation to protest against governments for totally free education and how could they achieve it;
After all, wouldn't it be good for one's own country to have educated citizens or subjects...?
Oh and there's lots and lots more in here;
I think this book is a "must read" for everyone;

******

Happy reading

So You Think You Know It All Huh...?
(Life's "short" Journey)

Chapter One

You know and I know and the rest of the world for that matter knows that, there are questions and questions in life, some we call big, some little, some cleaver some ordinary and yes, some stupid, some funny and some sad, some we think of our selves some we don't, and probably there's no question in this world that hasn't been asked from every one of us at one point of time or another;
The question not one of us ever asks is...
"How much travelling does a "man" in a lifetime"?
I mean really, can you stop reading this for a minute or so and think?
Can you come up with the answer or rather a figure...?
Well, believe it or not we spend near enough half of our entire

lives travelling; whether is to go to work and back, day trips, weekend breaks, visit our friends or relatives; and even at a young age we're always "on the go"; school, friends, parties, holidays;
Even when we come to a certain age we get encouraged to travel… walk as much as possible etc;
I mean is that ironic or what?
When were young our parents try almost anything to keep us indoors and when we grow old our "kids" will do almost anything for us to just get out, whether that is for our own good and I mean for exercise or maybe, they don't really want us "around" any more and yes, they do "throw" that at us, and they always come up with the same "phrase"
"It's good for you"
Let's take things from the beginning;
Ever since childhood or even earlier than that, from the day we were born; our parents prepare us for life's long journey and of course the
"Travelling" involved;

Let's take a mans life and analyze it a bit, and yes, I did say a bit because if I was to go into an "every day" detail thing… well, this book will never end;
But before that, I must emphasize that there are different ways of living;
There's what we call "western" ways, although some people call it "free world" and some even "intelligent"
There's the "Arab world"
There's the "Indian world"
There's the "Chinese world"
There's the "city world"
There's the "village world"
I mean I can go on and on here, all having there own ways and ways;
But let's just concentrate on the western one;
Even though only a few days old or young if you will, and the only world he knows is the mothers warmth, security and of course the pram;
The next thing on the agenda or your first lesson in life if you will, will be your preparation for life's long journey and to achieve

that… that means of course a lot of travelling;
Whether you like it or not, whether you eventually become a travelling person or one of those lazy bastards that prefer the armchair and never want to go anywhere, your early life lesson is a must and there's no two ways about it.
Of course even though you do not know what the word "scared" is yet, somehow you do feel it there and then when you will start recognizing or rather familiarize or even understand these two words "Going out"
Even though you know nothing yet of what is out there, your parents are indeed determent and eager to show you the world, get a taste of "what's out there"
But even though you will disagree with that, you have no say in the matter, after all, your mother wants to "show off" her baby for a the first couple of months…
And even though you know nothing yet, you sense fear… some kind of danger… and of course the only way to "protest" against that decision

is to scream your head off;
The fear of the unknown is
creeping up inside of you;
"What if you do not like what
you see out there"?
"What of all the dangers"?
"Are there any dangers"?
"Wouldn't it be a better idea to
stay indoors and the mother's
warmth and security"?
But who would take notice of what
you're trying to say anyway.
So, your first lessons are short
walks in the nearest park or
visiting friends and relatives;
Of course or rather eventually you
will like the going out "thing"...
What will make you want more of
the same are two things;
The first is you don't have to do
all the walking and that is the
fun of it all, you just lie there
and mom does all the work, your
job is enjoy whilst you discover
what the world is like around you;
colors, objects, sizes; and the
other is they and I mean everyone
you see for the first time is so
good with you, they're all smiles
and everyone seem to admire you,
and yes, they behave like "grown

up kids" as if they've never saw a
baby before, as if no one else
matters and even though that lasts
but a few brief moments every
time, you feel somewhat happy,
even though you are still to
discover what being "happy" is;
What will puzzle you is the "funny
lingo" they all use when they
speak to you;
That sort of "easy travel" will go
on for a couple of years or so
until other things take your
place, other things from now on
have more priority; this walks in
the park are no longer a
"Priority"
I mean you are no longer that
"cutie" any more;
It's like saying to you…
"That's it kiddo, we've done
what we had to do, from now on
you're on your own"
Of course you may not agree with
that decision, but hey, that is
it, take it or leave it; simply
because you are no longer that
little cutie thing any more, you
have become a pest in other words;
this is the time you start
screaming and screaming for

someone to take you out "walkies", but who could understand you, you see, you haven't yet mastered the lingo so, how can you stamp your authority?
That is probably the time when you begin to discover that "life sucks"; just as you started getting used to all this travel business too, and now that you feel you could walk the park all by your self, things started slowing down;
I mean halloo; you did not ask for this, they wanted you to… "Open your eyes"
Eventually you begin experimenting, breaking, smashing, destroying things; little things at first, just to size up the matter, see their reaction and if that doesn't work, then you go for bigger things to break, or maybe more expensive ones;
And to prove your point and stamp your authority, the minute someone takes you out walkies you are as good as gold; oh yes, that is the trick, that is your first real lesson only this time the roles are reversed, this time you are

the teacher;
They now know that if you were to stop screaming and breaking things, they better make time for your "travelling"
But you do not stop there do you?
As you grow older you begin to get sick and tired of this stupid park; I mean you know every inch of it by now, so you begin to wonder; oh yes; you are about to discover your first natural gift; "Imagination"...!!!
Wow...!!!
Little you may be but your imagination begins to come alive and grows bigger and bigger and not by the minute but by the second;
I mean you begin to wonder;
"What's around that bush"?
"What's around the corner"?
"What's on the other side of the street"?
"Who are all these people"?
"Why are they all in a rush"?
"Where are they all going"?
"Why is everyone crossing the road"?
"I want to do that too"...
And you want to make your "wonder"

a "reality"; so you try going that
way, but would they let you?
Fat chance of that happening;
So what one does in situations
like these?
Huh… that is the time were your
imagination awakes your inner
soldier and he goes almost
immediately to work;
First mission…?
Sneak away…!!!
The first thing you do is pretend
you're doing something innocent,
just to put everyone around you at
ease and when they're a bit
distracted, that is the perfect
time to "strike";
You simply sneak off, or rather
disappear is more appropriate;
You start wondering in strange
places, but before you get
familiar with the surroundings
some familiar face comes and grabs
you from behind;
That is when you actually want to
speed the process of speech
learning; that is the time were
you actually start demanding a few
things but, who can understand
your lingo?
You really want to say to

everyone;
"I only wanted to go around the corner and back, I was just curious what's there; that's all"
But your curiosity is what will get you in trouble…
This is where you see your mother's "other side", the other face… other character… one you haven't seen before; that is the very first time "sweet mom" will become "ugly witch" and have a real go at you;
From now on you will know that there are certain "rules" you have to abide by;
Of course you will put those so called rules to the test, time and time again, but you will discover that every time you do, you will be on the wrong end of the stick;
But in doing that, you will gradually come to understand two things;
One; it is the only way you will get attention and two; and this is where you will enjoy yourself, is breaking those rules… gets the "grownups" upset;
Of course the "breaking the rules" and getting away with it, will

last a couple of years more, until
you become four maybe even five
when your parents decide you are
indeed old enough to understand
and that is where the "fun" stops
and I mean period; that is where
the so called rules are
"enforced"…
"Light punishment" comes in… and
until you realise that they mean
business, the punishment gets
stronger and stronger;
Of course at the age of five or
so, your parents will begin to
"demand" from you a few things
too; learn the "lingo" as near
perfect as possible… learn how to
count at least up to ten… do the
"business" in the toilet and not
in your pants…
Once you master all those things,
they'll start preparing you for
the next stage of your life, and
of course that is, school;
Of course at the beginning you are
scared, maybe even think that
"school" is where they'll dump you
and never come back for you, but
they know an ingenious way to
"ease" you in…
They'll take you to "play school"

first, probably stay with you the first day or two so that you'll get use to it and yes, whether you like it or not, the first day or the second, you will find your self getting so use to your "new" playground, only because there are more kids your age and maybe they understand you more than your parents do; or you want to show them how things are done, show them how mucho you are, show them you're a born leader, show them who's boss;
The best part of it all is, in the new place you can do whatever you really like and get away with it too… your teacher wouldn't even dream of punishing you, not now days, if she does, huh, she'll simply loose her job; so gradually you get to like it there, you made some friends even though you did not get to choose them, you break things, you get to change the color of your clothes with all that painting and drawing AND get away with it, the teacher reads stories out for you, meals are always ready and on time; in other words, you never had it so

good…!!!
Little do you know that, at that age, all that… this wonderful and playful life you're having is just a trick, it is all "temporary"
They are preparing you for life's long journey that lies ahead of you; well, I should have said "short" really, because "life" is indeed short, never long enough, even if one lives a hundred plus;
I know it is really asking a bit much from someone young to understand that, oh no, when young or even young-ish… it is hard to "swallow" that fact, being young and all that, people think they'll "never" come to "that", that fact we come to understand only when we reach that age, or from what they call middle age, and when we do… we simply try to "hang on" for more… another year…month… week… day… or even as little as one more minute; for some reason, all living creatures just don't want to "let go"; but hey… that's another story, even though I think I do know why;
I think it has something to do with the "unknown"

We simply don't know what is after death, what is really waiting for us, or maybe even (like most people say) what kind of soul are we going to "surrender" come judging day;
Well, some of us people know what is "beyond that point" and one of those people includes me too;
You see, I have past away three times in my life and three times I came back, and yes, I do know what is "beyond"…….
I for one disagree with the words "past away" or at least in my case;
All I know is that the few minutes I was indeed "away", I found my self in a different world and the answer to your question you probably think is no, I never felt dead, I was very much alive;
And yes to your other question, which I am sure you are dying to ask; I did meet God and He is the One who sent me back and with a few "gifts" too;
But as I said, that is indeed another story, and if someone out there wants to know more about all that, all one has to do is buy the

first three novels of mine entitled
Saint Johnny Walker's (SJW) series and the books are;
1) (SJW) How To... Become A Saint
2) (SJW) My First Mission
3) (SJW) Return Home
And one could purchase them through the "net" at
www.lulu.com
www.amazon.com
www.google.com
www.barnesandnoble.com
Just print at the search button... Antonio Salacuri's books and you're there;
Although from the titles one would think it is all about religion and all that, well, I assure you, they are far from all that;
But I assure you also that, in reading theses books, they will indeed enlighten you... humor you... the suspense is unbelievable... your adrenaline will hit record heights;
Need I say more...?
And yes; they're all written in plain... simple... and down to earth English that everyone speaks, Brit or no Brit, no fancy words... that

one needs a dictionary to understand...
And yes; I promise you one thing, they'll change the way you think, the way you see the world, and maybe even your life;
So, back to "our" story
In other words they are making sure you will start getting used to the idea that "mamma" will not be around if and when you need her, well, at least for a few hours every day at first;
Any little problems you may face every day, you will need to "deal" with them your self.
And that is indeed the very first time you will feel the real meaning of the phrase...
"From now on "kiddo", you're on your own"
And that is indeed the beginning of "maturity"
That will be your very first test, your very first day of taking on responsibility of your own life;
Your very first day without "mommy" for protection

So You Think You Know It All Huh...?
(Life's "Short" Journey)
Chapter Two

Oh yes; that trick is simply to get use to the idea of being "out there"... get use to other people... mix with strangers... and gradually learn how to face the world on your own;
Of course you have no idea as yet about any if not all of all that, all you know at this stage is, life is only fun, fun and more fun and everything else around you works like clockwork;
In fact, the only thing you mite hate is the travelling to and from the kindergarten; you know... being tight down in the car with the seat belt, and being little you cannot see anything out there;
And this kind of travelling will go on and on, and it will seem for ever for you until, shall we say graduate from play school and start your proper school, your

first grade…!
Of course by now, your parents will try hard to find another house close to your school as possible, they would want to make their lives as easy as possible too you know; but you'll never hear them say or admit that; They'll come up with…
"It is better for the kid to be close to school"
Well, whether you agree with that or not, you find your self in a new house and… within walking distance from where you have to travel every day… and that "move" was done before you become six or there about; in other words before you get old enough to "sas" them out and I mean what their "plan" is for the very near future for you;
Of course being little still, one of your parents will drive you there day in day out and that is for the first year or so until you really get used the idea that for the next five or six years you would have to travel back and forth to the same school and all that…

After your first grade and of course your summer's family holidays and just before school opens its gates again your parents will brainwash you into taking the bus to and from school every day; oh they'll come up with...
"Look at all your friends, they're going with the bus and they're all happy and all that"...
Of course being naïve you wouldn't even think of the fact that your parents are indeed fed up with having to put you in their everyday schedule of driving you there every day; especially the picking you up... that is the "killer blow" for them; that part of travelling for them is, let's say, out of their way; they prefer to pay the monthly fee and have an extra hour to them selves...
And if you really think about it, you will discover that, from the day you board that bus... that is the day you will remember (when you grow old) your first bus ride, and on your own... Wow...!!!
That is the beginning of a new life for you...
That is the very first day you

will... "Face the world on your own"
You will travel to and from school
day in day out... week in week out...
month in month out and yes... year
in year out;
Not forgetting school outings,
weekend outings, summer holidays...
and that's a lot of travelling...
Although at the time your mind
will never "travel" enough to
realize the miles and miles you
will spend "on the go"
Why, I hear you ask;
Simply because you're so young and
your mind is pre-occupied with
other things, more important
things, and that is... fun-fun and
more fun; after all, you have an
entire life ahead of you to think
about other things;
It is only when you grow old and
"grey" that all that will "flash"
through your shrinking brain every
now and then and I assure you of
one thing at that age; you will
start talking to your self and
that is for two reasons;
One is that no one will talk to
you any more because you are
simply "old"
Two; the new generation always

think they know everything, so what could you possibly tell them that they don't already know...?
Especially now days with all these computers they all possess;
You will end up living a "lonely life"
Even if your wife is "still around" you will have nothing to talk about any more, not after so many years together;
But all that will come later, much-much later in life; but in saying that, don't think "much-much" means for ever, I assure you, before you know it, you're near "the end" and in some cases, life ends a lot quicker than we anticipate, and when that occurs we do not even have time to blink;
Not enough time to think or rather look back...
Here the one minute and gone the next;

So You Think You Know It All Huh...?
(Life's "Short" Journey)
Chapter Three

Of course as you grow older, this travelling will get more and more intense...
Some times because you have no say in the matter and some times you, your self will either demand... and some times... well, it's expected... more like tradition...
Some of these journeys you are indeed all for it, but some you're more or less forced into and that is when the devil in you will pop out and... well, you know what...
Especially if you're forced to visit some relatives who you hate their guts and for some reason you cannot refuse to go and having to sit with them for a while;
But you should be glad that, these kinds of "visits" are indeed few and far between, and yes, I do agree with you, I also find them unnecessary, if you do not like

them or enjoy their company;
I will even go as far as to say;
"Once, is once to many" and I do
mean the… visiting relatives;
I mean it is bad enough you
couldn't have chosen them and now
you have to visit them; "Isn't
life a bitch"?
Of course as you progress in
grades you can always find excuses
that you have a lot of homework
just to avoid these miserable
creatures; and that takes care of
that;
And one day… when you least expect
it, perhaps on your birthday, you
will get the best present you
could ever wish for…
"A bike" what…!!!
Oh the miles and miles you will
travel with that…
Freedom…!!!
The first few days you will
discover not only what your
neighborhood looks like but what
your town looks like; especially
if you gang up with other kids
with bikes; oh you will not
believe the travelling you'll do
with that bike;
Of course we all know that the

only way for you to leave the saddle will be either outgrow it or something more important will come your way, like a… girlfriend perhaps or more to "our recent times" a computer;
Yes, don't be surprised if your parents come up with a PC for you, just to get you "off the streets"
Well, now your life will take a turn… you'll do all your travelling with your fingers; once on the internet… sky is the limit;
Of course it will take you some time to… "Master it" and that is the time your parents will more or less "scream" at you to get out of that bedroom of yours;
Suddenly you find your self in high school and of course things in life are getting more and more serious;
Your parents of course still think you're a kid and of course you have a different opinion; nothing personal but you see, all kids at the age of twelve, thirteen or fourteen are confused; they are kids when doing chores and when convenient… and grownups when they need to be;

Of course the travelling to and
from school every day, only this
time the distance is somewhat
greater than before and the bus
ride to and from is still on until
the day you, your self will be
embarrassed from your friends and
ask for a bike again;
Of course your parents will gladly
buy you one and you'll think the
world for them for giving you this
present; but the truth is, the
bike is a lot cheaper for them
than the bus fare every day;
In other words you were doing them
a favor…
Now imagine if you travel with
your bike five or six or maybe
even seven miles a day, to and
from school and maybe to a
friend's house and back for the
next three or four years… I assure
you, that's a lot of miles…, a lot
of peddling… its like crossing the
entire Atlantic and back and
probably have a few miles to spare
too;
Of course lately "the fashion" are
these so called "fitness centers"
I mean halloo, don't you think
you're already fully "exercised"

with all this paddling you do every day?
Oh no… because everyone else does it, you're more or less "have" to travel every so often to the gym too; especially if you see someone of the opposite sex there that you fancied from day one you walked in there.
And that means adding more and more miles to your every day travel…
And if you think that is bad enough, wait till you start dating…
Aha… dating;
Now this is the time where things might get a little out of hand;
One could say, life moves to a different level;
Dating means spending, and spending means money, money you do not have;
Suddenly your weekly allowances are no way near enough and that means one of two things;
You either ask your parents for an increase which is a little embarrassing or you'll need a part time job of some kind;
That means adding more and more

miles every day to your travelling;
At this stage in your life you will realize that there are not enough hours in the day, your spare time you had every day, suddenly disappears;
Your life from now on becomes somewhat "full" if you will;
Everything you do from now on have to be carefully measured; and I mean in time consuming;
No room for any more "excitements"
But hey, let's face it, being a teenager and all that… means you could take it all, you think that there's nothing in this world you cannot do.
That is true in a way and let me assure you each and every "kid" of that age feels the same, only because the human brain is also a teenager and knows nothing about what life is really all about.
Even though travelling in general is consider to be fun, at this stage of one's life is beginning to feel the effects;
Not at the beginning of course but after a few weeks;
Don't forget, from the minute you

wake up, you'll be either on the
go, at school, home studying,
working for that extra money, on
the PC, or with the girlfriend;
A few weeks of that and you will
begin to "daydream" your bed, and
I mean every single minute you're
awake;

So You Think You Know It All Huh...? (Life's "Short" Journey) Chapter Four

For the next two or three years,
until you graduate from high
school you would be glad that,
that is all over, and of course
you would look forward to a
longish
and well deserved holiday; and
I mean the farther the destination
from wherever you are the better;
you just want to be as far away
from everything you know as
possible; maybe even travel to the
other side of the world if your
savings can take you there;
And yes; you would not give a toss
if you spend every last penny you
saved either;
But "reality" soon creeps up on
you and before you know it,
holiday time is over and... problems
start;
Little ones at first, but problems
nevertheless;

Your first and major one will be the decision you will make as to… do I listen to my parents and go collage…?
This is the time where you will need time for your self to make the big decision;
And trust me when I tell you; the decision is way-way bigger than you think; after all, your entire future is at stake;
Do you quit and look for a job…?
If yes, what can you do…?
What is available…?
How much will you earn…?
Will that be enough for…?
If I do that, will I ever be able to "better" my life or will I stay with a stupid wage until the day I die…?
On the other hand, if you choose collage;
Will you ask your parents to pay for it…?
Can they afford it…?
Maybe you could help towards the cost by taking a part time job…?
What of your girlfriend…?
Would she wait…?
And if all that are all well and good, what do you study;

What will you eventually become…?
What studies do you follow…?
Will you be good at it…?
What if you fail…?
But the bigger "puzzle" in your
mind will be… what if you pass all
that and even with flying colors…
what then…?
Do you carry on…?
University…?
How much will that cost…?
Maybe you will try and get a
scholarship;
That is it… get a scholarship;
That means one of two things;
Now days to get one of "those" you
need to either be extremely
"cleaver" and that means study
study-study… or be extremely good
in some kind of sport…
Either way, one has to go through
"hell" to achieve that;
If you choose the first… that will
mean cutting off all other
"activities" in your life so you
could study as hard as possible;
If you choose the second… that
will mean you will spend more and
more time either in the fields or
the gym and less and less time for
your studies; which means, if you

graduate from university, which you will and that is a guarantee from "them" will you feel that you deserved it…?
Will you feel confident enough to face the world with a "fake" certificate…?
With that certificate in your hands, will you feel you are ready to "face the world?"
Yes, I know what you'll say;
"A certificate is after all a certificate"
Or maybe even
"Anything is better than nothing"
Well, who can argue with that, but, will that give you confidence one needs for the near future to say the least to… really face the world on your own?
What a decision huh…?
The "stress" you will be under is indescribable to say the least;
One thing for sure; your imagination will travel you so far… maybe even to a different dimension until you come up with what you'll think is the right decision.
So as I said the next three or four years you will spend in a

collage and of course your parents will arrange for you accommodation close by so you will not have to travel all that far every day;
That is indeed a blessing for you, take my word on that; because of either your studying will be "intense" or your sports activities will have a real effect on you; what I am trying to say hear is either way these three or for years will make you feel so tired, you'll be more or less like a "zombie" you will look forward to some summer holidays, in fact a couple of months before the summer breaks you will think of nothing else.
Eventually you will do the right thing of course and end up in one; The travelling will be to the minimum thanks to mom and dad, but travelling nevertheless;

So You Think You Know It All Huh...?
(Life's "Short" Journey)
Chapter Five

Now that you're in collage you will find that collage life is a little different than the one you've experienced so far;
More responsibilities, let's just say... a lot is expected from you;
You have to come up in other words with "the goods" make sure you make your parents proud of you, but most important... your self;
The three or four years in collage will change you somewhat;
That is the time of your life where you will feel the change and I mean from being a kid to a man, and I mean if you're an ordinary looking guy;
But if you're one of those who were, blessed with good looks and especially with athletic build... huh... your troubles will just begin, and I do mean with the opposite sex... yes, the girls...!!!

I don't know whether having all those "gifts" are to your advantage or not, or let's say being fortunate or not, for me that matter could be "debatable" and I explain why...
Being popular with all "available and unavailable" girls are sometimes if not always a huge problem;
Of course you will find that out the hard way as we all say;
But as we all say… it's part of the process… part of growing up… part of life if you will and there's nothing you can do to either alter or change any of all that;
This is something you have to "pass through" in your life, like we all did;
Somehow, you will find a way to "make time" for all of them, at least at the beginning until you pick the right one you think is for you;
Bear in mind that usually when there's a lot to choose from, we tend to go for "looks" first and that could turn out to be a big mistake, and yes, we do end up

paying for our mistakes
Assuming you made the right choice, and you did pick the right one, can you really imagine how much travelling is involved here…?
How much of your valuable time you have to… just spent with her…?
Oh once they "grab hold of you", they "demand" and demand…
Trust me when I tell you; you will take this one out here there and everywhere… the other one… then the other and then the other…
Some will make you "sick" to your stomach but some will make you feel great being with and that is the problem;
You will be in at least two minds who to pick as the "right" one;
In other words, you will find that the day's twenty four hours are indeed not enough all of a sudden;
You will find that your days are so "full" there's hardly any room to breathe;
Class time… study time… meal time… girlfriend time… sports time…
But hey… you're in your early twenties; remember, you can do anything… maybe even think of everything too;

But by the end of every semester you would feel you cannot wait till you go home and just take it easy… just relax… just get away from everything;
But that of course involves more travelling…
Visit your old friends… maybe old girlfriend… trips with mom and dad at the weekends… have a proper holiday somewhere…
In fact, being a "grown up" now, you will get really tired of all these and cannot wait till you go back each and every summer break;
And suddenly you find your self graduating and of course with honors;
This is the day you will see your parents looking and probably filming you as you receive that certificate saying "bla-bla-bla" and yes, your mother crying;
That day will be for ever and ever at the memory bank of your brain;
You made it…!!!
You deserve a big "bravo" and you will want the entire world to know about it too;
The feeling you will get that particulate moment will be

indescribable… you will think you're walking on air…
Nothing and I mean nothing else matters in this world, you have indeed made it…!!!
Now you can do anything… concur the world if you choose to;
But that day will go and never come back, reality soon comes;
And when I say soon, I mean sooner than you think;
Oh you will have a few days to celebrate your "victory" alright…
Probable go on a longish holiday, a well deserved one at that too;
But that will come and go just like that and… that is where you will find your self facing yet another problem… a bigger problem…
And that is… you now hold a collage certificate, but what is it worth…?
What good will it do regarding your future…?
Let me assure you… nothing;
Who will employ you with that…?
I assure you, no one, not now days;
Now days they want to see PhDs… doctorates… even bachelors are not good enough.

In some cases having something
short of "masters" you are indeed
in trouble;
And that means one of two things;
You will have to make a decision
for your future;
Quitting "school" altogether and
get a job or carry on…?
Carry on means another four… five…
maybe even six years more pending
on what you choose to study;
If you choose the first one, that
will mean getting a… what people
call an ordinary job and with a
wage that could not support one
person let alone a family;
If you choose the second one…
well, those other questions will
pop up in your mind…
How long…?
How much…?
Where…?
What…?
And the bigger question is who
will pay the bill…?
"How long" depends on "what" you
what to become…
"Where" depends on many factors.
I.e. what marks you have on your
collage certificate…
"Space availability"

"What country"
As for the "how much"… well, your guess is as good as mine; I mean these universities are really unbelievable, they come up with such an astronomical some it is unreal;
Why governments around the world are indeed "allowing" these things…?
I think education in general should be free for all, regardless of or in what level;
After all, being highly educated is good for one's own country, is it not…?
As far as I am concerned, being well educated and successful, one will pay enormously to one's own country and I don't mean just in money or taxes but lots and lots more;
Mmm, maybe all students in the world should arrange simultaneously to "boycott" the schools and protest against this; I mean now days it is easy with this internet thing right…?
Halloo you guys out there… do something… isn't it time you lot to wake up…?

I mean don't look at me, I am way past that stage now, I wish I could turn the clock back, but that is somewhat impossible, but you...?
In my days there was no internet... no microchip... people were still amazed by "man on the moon" and even that was watched around the world on a black and white TV; and yes, we were indeed amazed how far technology was gone for us to see live pictures...!!!
Whatever computer was around those days were owned by big companies, and they were as big as one's own bedroom and, one maybe two people were allowed to use it, the so called "experts"
We never even dreamed of "digital" or a mobile phone;
But this day and age paying for education...?
My God people wake up;
Oups... I think I got a little carried away there... sorry... but hey; do you really blame me...???
Isn't education good for mankind...?
So why pay for it...???????
I know for some, getting into one of these "establishments" is easy,

"papa" can afford it and all that, but what about the rest…?
Being poor, or not so well off if you will, does not make one stupid;
I know and maybe the rest of the world knows that some of these "poor" families "produce" a "genius" every so often, and because of "poorness" they either go wasted or at most they delay their education for a number of years to work and save up;
What a waist of time I say…
Some poor parents are "forced" to take loan after loan to educate their offspring;
I even heard of a father selling a kidney, just so he can give his son an education;
Shame on governments, that is my opinion;
So… what are you waiting for guys?
Get up and GO…
Don't forget one important fact… your turn will come and a lot sooner than you think, and I mean for… educating your own kids;
Will you be able to do so…?
The more you delay… the more you will pay… pay… pay…

Oh I do not care if you even say it was all my idea, so long as you do it;
I assure you one thing;
It might take some time but...
YOU WILL SUCCEED;
Remember the old phrase...
"All good things... take time"
All you have to do is boycott one week; give "them" a couple of months to think about it then another week... and then another;
Then they'll know you mean business;
In my opinion, governments should STOP spending on weapons, and educate its citizens;
As far as I am concerned, even though it is somewhat late for me, it is all up to you if you want to succeed;
All I can do now is to encourage you "kids" and give you something to go by, and that is what my own father said to me about an hour before he died, but I was too little to understand it then;
I hope you will now;
And what he said was...
"Remember son, **All good things in this world we live in, are not**

really things"
And how right he was…!!!
I find that there are many of those "things" in life but the first two on my list are… life it self and of course education;
I do hope you all take my advice and do something about it;
But let's go back to our story;
It is obvious that one way or another you will end up going to university; if nothing else… you wouldn't want to "waste" all these years of collage would you…?
After all, this day and age we live in, is indeed the world of technology and computers and God only knows what's to come;
In other words, those were indeed the days were one could say…
"Oh I don't know, I'll go as an apprentice and learn a trade;
Oh no, that is indeed a thing of the past; now days "we" and I mean the western world think differently now; we live in a world of technology and higher education and we even found a way to fulfill the "empty" spaces;
Now days if we're in desperate need of workers, we simply import

them; the third world is indeed full of them and what's more, they come cheap too;
But that's yet another story;
So, you still have the summer break before all that remember?
This is the time were you will want to travel the world…
Well, as long a holiday as possible at least;
So you pick a long distance destination, somewhere exotic;
At this stage you don't mind the longish hours of travelling either because you feel after all you deserve it after all that "hard work" finishing collage;
But we all know the phrase "time flies" especially when you're having fun, so comes the day you'll be travelling all the way back and to reality;
Yes reality, these exotic places are just a fantasy world really and fantasy tends to wear out and the dream world usually ends a lot quicker than you think or more realistically hope for;
Even though this holiday and the fantasy world will take up permanent residency in your memory

bank… and no matter how many times you talk about your "adventures" there with friends and relatives or lying in your own bed and "re-dream" of all that and wish you were there still, the fact remains… you are now in
the "real world"
Oh I know, there's no harm in dreaming, or some will say "it costs nothing" but the sooner we realize that dreams are nothing but dreams, the quicker we adjust to the real world and of course the everyday problems that come our way;
Ha… If only we could live our dreams every single minute of every day huh…???

So You Think You Know It All Huh...?
(Life's "Short" Journey)
Chapter Six

That is the beginning of the next four or five year problems you'll be facing;
Finding the right university...
Choosing the right subject...
Will your first choice university accept you...?
Where to secure accommodation...?
How far will you have to travel every day...?
How will you travel...?
Can you afford a car...?
Public transport maybe...?
Will you get a room mate...?
Can you share your room with others...?
Will you get along...?
What if not...?
Would you just tell him "piss off"...?
Would you try and find another...?
Would the second one be "ok"...?
What if he is a noisy bastard and

you cannot study…?
What if he brings girls every day and you have to give him "space"…?
What if the subject you choose to follow is a bit harder than you first thought and it's beyond you…?
Would you risk loosing an entire year and start all over again on a different subject…?
I mean I can go on and on here, but I think you got the picture or where I am getting at;
Even though I've been there and gone through all that and I mean knowing what you will go through physically and mentally, and one could say I am more the wiser now, I still would not volunteer to change places with you at that stage of your life.
All I can say to you is "good luck" with your decisions, but as an advise I would say, think long and hard… and I do mean long and hard, after all, the decision you come up with, concerns your entire future;
Once you have made your decision that is it… there's simply not going back… no changing your mind

half way through either.
And to prepare your self, you obviously want to pay a visit to the university, the town… the supermarket… the library and all the rest before moving there;
So before you know it, you'll travel there and check everything out, probably with your parents too, after all they will want to be sure and be at ease as well that their boy will be safe and all that… you'll be happy and most certainly ok;
Once happy and satisfied you'll travel all the way back home and of course prepare your self for what is to come mentally too;
And time is not on your side for a change… before you know it, ready or not it will be time for the big move;
Yes; I do call it the big move, after all, whatever lies ahead of you in the next three or four years, whatever certificate you come up with or rather "earn" will be your future and I mean your entire future…
Once you make the "move" that is it… no turning back;

From now on you will find or rather discover that even your way of thinking will somewhat change; that will be the sign… the sign of adulthood;
Of course every now and then you will think like a kid and behave like one too, after all whether you agree with it or not you are still a kid really; but the time will come that you will realize that being a kid is really behind you now and concentrate on being an adult and of course finish what you started with and with as high marks as possible;
No more play-play and work, that will change to work-work and maybe play;
Once you realize that you will somewhat rearrange your every day activities, travelling… down to the minimum, sleep… down to the minimum, less going out… less fun… less girls… that is the time you'll know you're "maturing"
From now on it's more and more study;
You will end up more or less like a zombie; you will look forward to a longish summer break and of

course that summer holiday
somewhere;
No; I do not blame you really,
after all you're still a young
man, full of life and being in
that six by nine room of yours day
in day out studying, you will feel
like a prisoner; well, more like
in one of those what they call
open prisons;
When eventually "summer break"
comes you will want to travel
everywhere… see everyone you know…
tell everyone…
"Halloo I am still around" and
that is for the first few days,
after that your mind will be on
travelling and having fun-fun-fun;
But as I said before, time flies
when having fun, so before you
know it… it is that time again;
Time to go through "hell" again;
Time to go back;
And that will become a "regular"
thing for the next few years;
Year in year out, you are
"sentenced" to nine or ten months
a year imprisonment, at least that
is how you will eventually see it;
Some times you will even think
that the "open prison" will feel

more like "solitary" or even worse "forced labor" but what can one do really, you will eventually come to terms with all that and actually say to your self;
"I went to the ball room, I might as well dance"
Although these few years in university will feel like a life time, you will soon discover that they're gone… finished… they're all behind you;
The day you will graduate will be forever in the back of your mind; It will be THE day…
A memorable day indeed…!!!
Your day and no one can take that away from you…
Even though you have indeed suffered a lot to reach there, in later stages of your life you will wished you were back there, only because life is not really what we all expect or wish for;
I know that life is not what it is but what we make out of it, but, no one in this world can "program" it, no matter how many plans we do;
Life is not a "play" that you rehearse time and time again so

you'll get it perfect;
Life has its ups and downs...
And I assure you there are more
down than ups;
That is why life is a wonderful
"thing" really, one never knows
what lies ahead; laughter...
happiness... adrenaline at its
highest and lowest... misery... fears...
dangers... unexpected things...
unknown things... mistakes... lots of
mistakes...
Illnesses... accidents... parties...
marriages... divorces... families...
children... deaths... travelling... more
travelling... and yes more
travelling;
One should expect the unexpected...
The list is so big, I can go on
and on here... but I am sure you got
the message or rather the picture;
all you have to do is... think a
little and you're there;
But; at this stage in your life,
life is so wonderful you would not
give a shit about any of all that;
And yes, I for one would not blame
you, after all, you are still in
your mid twenties... still feeling
as young... still full of energy
even though you are indeed tired

from all that "ordeal" but having in your possession that certificate makes all the difference;
The only things in your mind now are two things;
Show off your "achievements" in other words make sure all who know you, know that you've "made it" you have reached your goals;
And the other is a well deserved long-long holiday;
Even though you will hear time and time again the…
"What are you going to do now?"
Even though you know "they" have a point… you would not give a shit about nothing really because of the longish and well deserved holiday that's in your mind;
Of course you know and I know and yes, the rest of the world knows that, that will be over too and you'll be coming back and yes, back to reality;
That is the time where you will start thinking like a grown up, everyone around you expects you to too; everyone awaits your decision as to… what next; well, at least that is what you'll feel they

think, what is your next move;
You on the other hand will feel you know enough to take on the world...
So after the few days rest... come THE pressure, and even though no one asked any questions yet, you will get this feeling that, time of "rest" is long gone and people around you are looking at you in a weird way, as if their look has a question or two in there;
That's when you'll say to your self "it is time" time to face the world;
In other words, time to get a job... a real job;
So you start applying for a few... You will travel here there and everywhere for interviews;
And, unless you know someone who knows someone who in turn know someone and get a position straight away, otherwise...???
On the other hand, if you are one of those who know no one, and I mean one of those so called "important" person, well, this is where you will realize the meaning of the phrase "Welcome to the real world"

You will end up travelling here there and everywhere for interviews and interviews, day in day out and the answers you will get are… "We'll let you know"
Oh some of these "firms" will offer you the position straight away, but the money they'll offer will be a lot lower than you could imagine, and the excuse will be the same every time…
"Not enough experience" if not "No experience at all"
You will get the feeling of humiliation time and time again with what they offer;
You will think that all these years of hard work behind the desks were a waste of time and money;
Many sleepless nights thinking and thinking;
Days in days out… sleepless nights in sleepless nights out;
No matter what you think and do seem to be a waste of time and money;
And the worse of it all… you will feel the pressure, pressure from your family… pressure from your friends… you will even feel the

pressure from your neighbor… you will think that even he is looking at you in a weird way;
The days and days you'll lock your self in your bedroom, and not because you like it there, oh no, it is because you'll be somewhat embarrassed from your own family;
After all, you are a grownup now and being jobless and penniless is not a nice feeling to say the least;

So You Think You Know It All Huh...?
(Life's "Short" Journey)
Chapter Seven

Eventually you'll come to a major decision;
You'll apply to everything you can think of, anything is better than nothing;
Of course the end result will be landing a job that you're over qualified for and that some times is frustrating to say the least, because you will be getting orders from an idiot and I mean the boss;
But, what can you do...?
Anything is better than nothing, after all you need the job, shut everyone up and there's some money coming in too;
Not forgetting the old phrase...
"Beggars cannot be choosers"
Oh the times you will say that to your self...!!!
But there's another old phrase, a Latin one that goes...
"Toom-Spiro-Spero" and that means

"As long as I breathe… I hope"
Yes, you will hope that while you are "slaving" for an idiot that does not or rather never appreciates your work, one or two of your applications you filled for a better position in life will eventually come through;
Meanwhile, although you feel you are indeed wasted there you stick to that and yes… you travel every so often after work, in search for something better;
One thing for sure though, this job will "mature" you, make you more the wiser; in other words, it will bring you down to earth, you will come to realize the well known fact that… "Life stinks"
From now on any decisions you make you will find that they are indeed more on the mature side, probably think twice each and every decision you take; don't forget, you are pushing thirties by now;
And the closer you get to the big thirty the wiser you get;
Being a little lucky in your life for a change, one of your applications will come through and yes, you land the job you always

wanted, or at least the one in your field, the one you have studied all these years;
Money is not bad, or at least a little better than from the last job; at least for the first six months or a year, you get to travel, probably representing the company you work for, all expenses paid etc…
Oh at the beginning you will think you are the luckiest person in the world, everything around you is working like clock work;
But, soon you will discover that all this travelling is really a slow killer; the delays… the waiting in airports… the coffee's you will consume…
Especially lately;
Ever since nine-eleven;
You cannot take this with you… you cannot take that with you…
The people in the airports look at you as, first as a criminal or rather as a terrorist first and then as a proper and respectable human being;
Huh… the last time I had to travel by air, I promise my self I will never travel by air ever again or

at least avoid it as much as possible;
I felt humiliated when I went through the hand luggage check at Heathrow airport, when I was asked to remove my shoes and belt to, as I went through that checking "thing" whatever they call it, that "blips" every time you go through whether you carry anything metal or not and yes; I went through "physical" body check too; I don't know about you or anyone else out there but every time that happens I feel not only humiliation but disgust too;
What I am trying to say here is…
"A man is not only touching me all over, but feeling every pert of me, and I allow him to do it, or rather not allowed to refuse, and that to me is like being submitted to a gay act whether one is gay or not, and trust me, if one is "straight" or not gay if you will it is indeed very and I do mean very upsetting"
And to make things even worse or rather to make you feel worse, there's always an audients around you, there's the fellow travelers

behind you, you are in the center standing in front of this security guy arms high and wide, legs wide apart, and a lot of his colleagues are standing on both your left and right and admire the show;
One feels like being the star of the 3D show;
And let me assure you, I was not the only one feeling bad;
Personally I disagree with all that, I don't mean of course the security checks and all that, I do know it is all for our own good etc, but if one thinks a little, one would find that if a terrorist would want to "blow up the place" he or she can do it very easy;
All he/she need is a couple of bags full of explosives and ignite them up before boarding the aircraft, at the check in counters;
Halloo… all the security is focus or concentrated on the aircraft's safety and not at the ground;
What if something like that really occurred…?
I am sure you could imagine the "damage" AND the deaths…
And if I… a humble and quiet

person thought of "it" I am sure
some of these so called terrorists
thought of it too;
I hope the "officials" will do
something about that;
Surely at this day and age and
with all that technology
available… will come up with
something to prevent disasters
like these ever happening;
And if I can think like that,
surely terrorists could to;
I would suggest these so called
scientists in the world to focus
their research in finding some
kind of a warning system or devise
that detects explosives or gun
powder or whatever, strategically
placed one or two miles or
kilometers around every airport,
warning them of any of that, long
before they approach terminals and
of course people;
I for one, every time I fly or I
even visit an airport to see
someone off, I always have this
funny idea or rather this fear
that this is my last day on earth,
and yes, I do not think
governments around the world are
doing enough to make me think or

feel otherwise, not with today's technology;
Would anyone actually disagree with me…? I wonder.
First of all the airports will be clear of guns… armed police… armed security… after all it is not only "ugly" if I was permitted to use that word but it is not only the ugliness, there are also children travelers too; does anyone out there know what is in a child's mind when he/she being happy that they'll travel for fun let's say and see the airport full of fully armed men…?
And when I say fully armed I mean they carry enough on them to start a war;
Huh… those were indeed the says were travelling was considered fun; now days is anything but; at least that is my opinion;
Oups… I think I got a bit carried away there, sorry…
But hey… do you blame me…?
I am so… against guns, I even have a go at the toy shops who sell toy guns, and of course the parents who buy them for their children; in fact I was thrown out of these

shops many a time too;
But that is another story;
Let's go back to the original;
As I was saying, life will become more and more boring… tiring… maybe even miserable after a while;
Seeing and doing the same things over and over again tends to tire people and that is when you will either ask for a "desk job" or a transfer or even look for another job;
So you start looking and looking for a better one, if there's such a thing "better"
If the company you work for really appreciate you, they'll come up with something;
If on the other hand they refuse… well, that's one way of knowing what they think of you;

So You Think You Know It All Huh...?
(Life's "Short" Journey)
Chapter Eight

After a long and hard straggle you do land the job you've always wanted;
Of course you think your luck has finally changed but let me assure you, luck has nothing to do with the sudden change in your working life, there are two factors here; that university certificate you've earned and your age;
People see you as a mature man now, more let's say responsible and all that;
After all you are now in your thirties and although you still feel young-ish, you, your self will see the different way people talk and behave towards you;
After settling down in your new job and things go the way you want your mind will start thinking of having your own family;
Oh yes, trust me you will;

Even though you heard a lot about marriages and divorces and everything bad there is to hear about that, you still go ahead and do it anyway;
And that is the biggest mistake you will ever do;
Don't get me wrong, having a family of your own is a wonderful thing, but, now days is more or less a guarantee that it will end in a divorce and some times even a lot quicker or sooner if you will that you think;
In my days, divorce was indeed unthinkable, however good or bad or even a miserable marriage one had; I my "old days" we had this idea if one want to call that, that… every one in this world will point their finger at you and saying… God really knows what… today things are completely the opposite, when people hear that one couple is "still" married after twenty years or even as little as seven or eight, is indeed a miracle let alone thirty or forty;
But, being human means masochists and whatever and whenever people

try to advice us what not to do,
we do exactly the opposite;
We simply have to learn the hard
way;
We simply go ahead and do it
anyway, even though we know
beforehand the outcome;
But for the sake of argument let's
say everything goes well and none
of the above comes your way;
Let's call you one of the lucky
ones;
Let's just call your case an
exception;
You found the right girl;
Everything seems to work like
clock work;
Well, that is all well and good or
so far so good if you will;
But allow me to inform you, your
troubles are just beginning and
yes, even with that so called
happy marriage;
And I mean your troubles as a
responsible adult has just begun;
From now on every decision you
make or take should be double and
even treble checked;

So You Think You Know It All Huh...?
(Life's "Short" Journey)
Chapter Nine

First and foremost, once you get married your life does not belong to you any more; and that is indeed a fact whether you agree with me or not;
Especially when you have children;
Everything you do from now on you have to think of your family first;
But let's take things from the beginning;
You didn't listen to everyone's advice about marriage or you decided against everyone's opinion and wanted to go ahead anyway;
Do you have any idea of how much it costs, and I mean just those couple of weeks before the ceremony...?
The travelling involved is unreal... getting the license... arranging the party... inviting friends... inviting relatives... running around for the

wedding dress... not forgetting the bridesmaid... the groom... finding old school pals... maybe even old teachers... colleagues from your work place... old colleagues... rehearsals... minister...
In other words you will find your self in a "spot of bother" to say the least;
Time and time again you will think "Is it really worth it"
But, don't forget, you are no longer just the one person, there's your fiancée around and she wants everything to be as near perfect as possible;
You cannot blame her really, after all you two will be married just the once in your lives so... you just give in, as we say;
But that "giving in" will turn to a boomerang I assure you;
After the ceremony your wife will know your weakest point... she'll know how to "handle" you;
You gave in once and that was enough for her;
She'll know what button to press so everything will go her way; and the only thing you will end up doing is... just shut up and go

along with her; and that is for two reasons;
First because you love her and don't want to hurt her… and the other is the other problems you are now facing… how expensive life is and to top it all up, you took on a mortgage for a house;
Now that is the real killer;
Taking on a house mortgage is worse that getting married to two women at the same time;
First of all, whatever savings you have will vanish from the minute you put that signature of yours on that piece of paper in the bank;
Second, give or take, half your salary will disappear before you know it for payments;
Third, the bank will be part owner of your house until you become an old man or to be more precise you do not own any little corner of what you think its your house until every last penny is paid; and let me assure you, they mean business, even once you delay payments and they'll hit you with everything they have;
But for the sake of argument, everything works fine with the

pair of you;
You both go to work… two incomes come in…
So the usual thing after that is decorating the house with the very latest and of course buying things that are really useless and I mean useless things for this wall and that wall, this corner and that corner, very expensive electrical and electronic "toys"
Of course to get all that you start running around in shops;
And no matter how many things you get and feel that the house is full, there's always room for more and more;
And before even moving in your new home you will need a new car, so you trade in your old for a new, but remember, there's your wife to think about too; so she does the same, after all, it is somewhat embarrassing to have your wife driving an old banger is it not…?
In other words or to put it in a simpler way, you're in the shit;
Up to your eye balls in dept, but hey… who cares right…?
You are living "A life of a luxury", you are both young

enough, both working;
Even though your monthly wages are disappearing before you see any of it, you think its ok really; you are still young enough to take it all;
But that "young enough" will not last long for one and on the other depths are building up, if not "mounting up"
And if that is not bad enough, one morning you get the surprise of your life;
Your wife announces something that will make you jump for joy…!!!
She says;
"Darling, I'm pregnant"…!!!
Oh you will jump for joy alright, that is for sure;
Your own kid is coming… your own offspring… carry on the tradition and all that;
But almost immediately many things will "run" through your mind;
"How the hell did that happened"…?
"I thought I was "careful"
"Maybe it's not mine"…
But whether you like it or not, whether you're ready to have a kid or not, this is it;
From now on everything you think

or talk about is for the kid;
From now on the kid has priority,
even though he or she hasn't come
to this world yet;
Travelling to the doctors more
often than you think… making sure
your wife does not have a hard
time in the house, you decide to
do a lot of housework… but soon
you will decide that "housework"
is not for you so, you take on a
maid instead;
You know what that means of
course, more expenses…
And before you know it, your wife
comes and says…
"It is too much for me, can't cope
I'll have to quit work"
Of course you know what that
means, expenses are raising and
less income…
Now everything depends on your
wages; mortgage… bills… food…
maid… clothing… doctors… cars…
petrol… take away… supermarket…
you name it, everything out of
your pay-package;
Trust me, all that will drive you
crazy;
You will soon find out that no
matter how much you earn it is

simply not enough;
So, what can you do…?
Simple, you pay a visit to your friendly bank manager for a loan;
But with all these expenses you have it is next to impossible to get one, so, you do the next best thing;
Re-mortgage your house;
And the money you will get will almost immediately disappear;
Oh yes they will…
You will be persuaded to decorate and furnish the baby's room;
If you're expecting a boy, everything will be in blue and if a girl all pink;
From now on things will get harder and harder, no extra money for anything else;
Needless to say that "outings" with friends are a thing of the pass;
You will even ask or rather beg for some overtime at work and if that is out of the question, you will start looking for part time work, anything really, so long as extra money comes in;
Oh you will travel and travel every day just to make a few

"pennies" extra for your family;
Suddenly you will find your self
working hours and hours to meet
ends mead;
And the closer the day of your
first born the harder you will
work;
Don't forget hospitals costs and
when I say costs, I mean an arm
and a leg and some times even
more; you see, there's no hospital
in the world that has a "price
list" displayed anywhere so people
can read before going in, they
charge whatever they want;
Of course the closer "the day" the
more visits to the doctors and
that means you will have to make
time for taking your wife there
and let me assure you, you do not
pick or choose the time or date
either, whenever or whatever the
doctor says or at his convenient,
and that is whether you can make
it or not… like it or not;
Now if you think that after having
the baby everything will go back
to "normal"… well, think again;
Let me assure you that your so
called "troubles" are about to
begin; the minute that baby comes

to this world, you, yes you, will be a changed man, forget the man you were, everything about you will change, the way you think… the way you talk… and nine out of ten times, the subject of your conversation will be your offspring;
Oh you will be so proud of your self… and yes, you will feel different too;
First of all you will travel to great lengths to please your wife for bringing your boy or girl to this world and I mean whatever she asks of you;
And if for one moment you think that was a bit expensive… tiring… and whatever else you care to add there, wait till you hear what that little one costs;
First and foremost, the baby's room has to have the proper "décor" and I don't mean furniture and all that, that you have done already, I mean little things like "flying butterflies, things that make sounds, colorful objects"
You name it should be in that room; and that is just for starters;

Those are the things you buy once and I mean for the first year;
Of course there are things you will need to buy every day or maybe on a weekly basis, and to start with… how about the baby's milk;
Yes, I do know what you're thinking right now and that is "breastfeed" yes?
Well, the sooner you forget that idea the better is for you;
Now days the breastfeed is a thing of the past; now days the ladies think of… not to "spoil" the shape of their breasts;
Now days everything is made easy for them;
The point is or rather the bad news for you at least is… every woman after giving birth produces milk and if they do not breastfeed they'll be in trouble, so what do they do…?
Simple, they visit the doctors for a period of time and he in turn prescribes medication for that or to put it simpler, to "dry out"
Halloo… one guess as to who is paying for all that and to add to all that, you will pay for either

a baby sitter for the time and
every time your wife travels to
and from the doctors;
In a way, that could turn out to
be a blessing really for you, and
I explain;
If your wife decides to
breastfeed… that will eventually
"alter" her breasts and now days,
all women are into this… "Silicon
implant" and guess how much that
costs;
But let's go back to the daily
expenses; the baby needs to be fed
every two - three hours, and that
is a lot of milk, and of course
every time the baby drinks milk he
or she will need changing… and
that means you will or rather he
or she will go through an entire
package of nappies or dippers or
whatever other name you care to
name them;
Have you any idea of how much they
cost…?
Try adding to that the travelling
to the supermarket every other day
to buy them…?
And not forgetting the time
consuming; time you can ill
afford, and no, don't even think

that your wife will do that, she'll be too weak to drive for at least the first month, the maximum she'll do will be a short walk in the park with the baby, and that is for the baby to "get some fresh air", well, at least that is the excuse, the truth is… she's dying to show off her baby to everyone;
Then you have the visits to the "centre" or more commonly known as the center, where parents take their infant for a quick check up and weighing;
And that is more travelling to and from there than you think;
But for the sake of argument, you go pass that stage and the baby is around three to four months old or young if you like;
That is the time where the mother (after everyone's advice) will introduce to the baby different food;
Of course she'll start from fruits;
She'll go to the supermarket and buy the most expensive little jars available;
Now every time you go to the supermarket the first thing on the

list will be these little jars for the kid;
And let me assure you, they're not cheep and it is not just the one kind or make;
There are hundreds of them;
You will start looking at the price tag instead of make, but your wife will have other ideas;
After all, she'll want the best for her baby and no one can blame her for that, so you go along with what she says anyway;
And people in general now days do not read what the label says, they just go for the most expensive ones, thinking that if it's expensive… it must be good;
Of course you will start the kid with liquidized fruit at least once a day so the baby will get use to it and gradually increase the dosage…
Then comes the real "solids" chicken, meat, veggies…
And if you think for one minute that your troubles are over… ha, think again;
If you thought that sleepless nights are a thing of the past, wait till you see from now on;

The kid will grow at an alarming rate now;
The body of a baby goes through hell if one can call it that;
The entire body goes through what they call "metamorphosis"
In other words every little part and I mean interior and exterior of the human body is "expanding" and I mean constantly;
The kid will scream all night, and who can blame him or her;
The muscles are growing by the minute if not by the second and that must hurt something terrible;
It is like someone "stretching" you while you are asleep to such an extent just so you will be a few milometer's taller and that is day in day out, night in night out, or should I say… 24/7
And if you did not get the picture yet… let me put it to you in a different way;
Imagine going to the gym and push your self "beyond" the limit, day in day out and I mean not just an hour every day, I mean being in the gym and pushing "beyond" your limits every minute of the day 24/7, and as for sleep, one or two

hours from pure exhaustion;
In this case I think the proper
phrase for this is…
"No pain no gain"
But of course today's generation
does not know things like that,
they only hear the kid screaming
from all that pain and the first
thing they do is "call the doctor"
As if he/she has this magic wand
and will "speed" the process;
And that is your first big mistake
regarding your offspring;
That is the first time the kid
will be introduced to drugs, and
why…? Because you want to sleep;
That "sleep" will cost you an arm
and a leg in money, but the real
damage will be on the poor kid;
As the kid grows you drug him/her
over and over again so you will
have peace and quiet… sleep at
nights;
Oh we are good in giving lectures
and all that… telling the kid to
keep away from drugs as he/she
grows up and start facing the real
world, but, halloo… we were the
first to introduce them to these
so called "bad habits"
Now days they all say that it is

the best thing for a baby, easing the pain a little and bla-bla… God almighty; we might as well pour a pint of beer down the baby's throat every night, I am sure that will do less damage than any drugs;
I mean these pharmaceutical companies will say anything to sell, or to put it more realistic, they'll advertise and advertise for you to buy… buy… even though some times we do indeed know that there's no "cure" and yet, with all that "bombardment" of advertising we all "fall" for it;
Example, I hear you ask…?
OK, here's a little one;
"Common cold"
We all know that technology is no way near that, and yet, we take this… that… and the other for it;
Result…?
The result is simple; we just delay the process;
As for the "ready made baby food" I don't know whether you agree with me or not, but, let's just analyze this a little;
Let's say you liquidized an apple or a banana or any other fruit and

keep it in the refrigerator for a
week or two;
Would you eat it after two weeks?
First of all, if it's not
"stinking" by now its color alone
will put you off;
And yet, these manufactures are
insisting that the contents of
every little jar is "pure" no
added this and no added that;
How the hell is that possible, I
would and I'm sure you would to
very much like to know;
God only knows what they put in
there to keep for so long and if
one checks the dates…?
Ha-ha-ha… these jars have a life
spam of maybe a year or two;
And yet; we do trust "them" and
not only give to "our" babies but
we also have this bad habit to…
force-feed them too; and why do
"we" do that… because we have this
idea that it is good for our kids;
One thing I will never understand;
"man" or better still, "the human"
race is suppose to be the superior
"being" in this world and that
makes me wonder some times;
Are we really…?
I mean a simple thing like what to

feed our own children became
"modernized" everything the modern
way, everything easy;
I suppose the next thing on
everyone's mind would be… sitting
on our armchair and using the
remote control to… "Grow the
children up"
I mean who knows, the rate
technology is progressing… the
phrase "Anything is possible" is
near enough out and a new phrase
come in, now they say "Everything
is possible"
"We're easily brainwashed" by some
cleaver bastards out there as to
what and how;
I mean we all know that these
people (if I can indeed call them
that) the only thing they have in
mind is to make more and more and
yet, we fall for that or rather we
refuse to think of that, "we", for
these people are "easy pray"
And yet, we like to call our
selves all sorts of names like…
superior… or worse, "intelligent"
If that is intelligence I don't
know what intelligence is;
Oups… I did get carried away again
didn't I…? Sorry; but really, just

think about it, would you or maybe
even could you blame me for
thinking like that…?
But for the sake of argument…
let's say you went along with this
and follow orders from the Mrs;
This "process" will go on for a
couple of months until… the kid is
ready for yet another change, this
time the baby is at an age to move
to "solids" and in saying that,
don't even think that the baby
will share whatever you eat or
whatever is in the pot, oh no… you
will continue buying from the
supermarket little jars, specially
made for infants, and when you see
the variety there is, you'll go
crazy;
I assure you it is like having a
menu with well over a hundred plus
pages to choose from;
But the worse part is that you are
not allowed to look even at the
prices or the only way you wont
get in to trouble with the Mrs. is
to go for the most expensive ones;
But I still insist, how it is
possible to go along with this
"theory" the manufactures are
telling us, "no added this… no

added that… pure this… and pure that"…
I mean if we cook any kind of food for our selves, and with the best ingredients, keep it is the refrigerator for a couple of days or so, and no matter how well we manage to seal it, maybe, just maybe that will still be good enough for human consumption up to a week or so;
And yet, we still believe these morons who, as I mentioned before, there's one thing only in their minds and that is to make money and we buy-buy-buy;
The worse part is, governments around the world lately are "bombarding" us with… and I quote; "Make sure of the expiry date" Unquote… what about the date it was made or cooked to be more precise…?
Has anyone out there actually read the "manufacturing" date…?
I really wonder at the end of the day… who is really the moron here…?
Halloo… just think about it, we are feeding our own children with all these "shit" and yet we have

the idea that we are doing what's
best for them;
If that is not a bad joke I don't
know what a bad joke is;
But for the sake of argument, and
just like everyone else out there
you're either one of those
"brainwashed" people and believe
whatever these money-grabbing
people write on the labels or
because you are indeed "scared" to
say or do something about it, you
opt to go along with what the Mrs.
say, just for your own convenient…
peace and quiet;
And if you think that by doing all
that your troubles are over, ha-
ha…think again;
Usually, before the baby is a year
old, he/she will have to go
through illnesses like "mumps" and
let me tell you, the baby will
suffer something terrible
throughout these weeks, not
forgetting all that about the body
stretching too at the same time,
and as for you, you will suffer
even more, only because you'll
feel helpless and all that;
And yes, before you know it, the
kid will get "measles" and the

suffering will start all over again;
And to top it all up, the kid will start "teething"; ha now there's something to keep you occupied all night;
The times you will travel to the doctors and back… the times the doctor will visit you… the miles and miles you will walk with the baby in your arms going through the entire house trying all sorts of things to take the baby's mind off the pain;
Halloo… no need to guess who is paying for all that;
But somehow, I am sure you will find a way in passing through this crisis too;
Of course by now you are almost broke and yes, you start feeling the effects… although still in your early thirties, you'll some times wake up in the morning feeling at least ten or even twenty years older;
All these "circumstances" will last until the baby becomes more or less a couple of years old;
That is the time where you'll think your troubles are indeed

over;
Well, it all depends how you look at it really;
Although your kid is now off the dippers… off the baby food… off the major sicknesses… and you think or rather say "thank God for all that"… here comes the unexpected;
Your wife comes and says…
"You know darling those stretch marks, I need plastic surgery to remove them"
Now here comes the hard part;
If you say "no" you're running the risk of a divorce and that is to put it mildly;
If on the other hand you give in and say "yes" the damage in your pocket will be so bad it will set you back so much, you would need to re-mortgage your house to pay for it;
So what does one do in situations like these…?
Simple, you "delay" it and I mean you'll find many ways of doing just that;
First you will come up with…
"Are you sure it's a good idea"?
Then, "we'll see"…

But the Mrs. is determent and
eventually you will give in but
still delaying it as much as
possible;
You'll come up with…
"We must find a good doctor, check
him out first, see examples etc"
Then you'll come up with…
"Let's not rush into this, see
another one"
And then of course another;
But sooner or later you'll run out
of excuses and guess what…?
Your wife will become so
frustrated or pissed off with you
she'll become a different person
than the one you married;
Most likely she'll start by giving
you "the silent treatment"
You'll try and try to explain to
her that the cost of having an
operation like that is really
astronomical and you simply cannot
afford it right now, but would she
listen or understand…?
The truth of the matter is that
she does not give a shit of how
much… all she cares about is
having it done here and now;
And if the silent treatment does
not have an affect on you, then

she'll try laving you without dinner;
Oh trust me, that is and will be every woman's "specialty";
Things will start being a little different from now on;
She'll move to "plan B"
You'll come home thinking dinner is waiting for you but instead… you'll settle for a sandwich, the very next day it will be one of the same, day three you'll know there's nothing to eat at home so you grab something on the way;
Well, let me assure you, that will be the biggest mistake you've ever do or done;
This time the lady of the house did cook something, just to spike you, and the minute you walk in the house you'll see your dinner on the table;
Of course the entire thing will end up in the bin and that is the minute you say…
"Sorry darling, but had something on the way here" and before saying "I'll eat it tomorrow"
The very next day you'll stay hungry again because you'll think she cooked for you;

But fat chance of that happening,
not after last night's
"performance"
This situation will be on for a
few weeks;
You'll end up eating out every
night but only half as much as you
need to survive, just in case she
does cook and don't want to
disappoint her again...
Of course by now you are so use to
this, you carry on as if nothing
changed;
The Mrs. on the other hand has
other ideas;
She'll know that plan B did not
work so she'll move to "plan C"
Plan "C" is every woman's
favorite;
From now on my dear friend you'll
find that she moved to the baby's
room, from now on you sleep alone;
Of course plan "C" does not mean
the rest are in order, oh no,
plans "A" "B" and "C" are still on
and will be on until you give in;
The sleepless nights you will have
thinking... and thinking... how long
is this going to go on...?
Oh you'll try to reason with her,
time and time again, but you know

it is indeed a lost battle;
So you'll leave it at that for a
while, hoping against hope that
she'll come to her senses;
But instead, you'll find that she
also has a plan "D"; and that is
"the killer blow"
You'll wake up one morning and
find her in the kitchen waiting
for you, just to say...
"I want a divorce"
Now why do women do that I'll
never know;
They'll "hit" you when you least
expect it;
I mean she had all night to come
and tell you, but no, they want to
make sure you'll hurt all day
thinking about it;
So, what one does in situations
like these...?
Do you give in or get a divorce...?
And to make things even worse,
they don't even want an answer
straight away, oh no... the first
thing they'll do is pick their
suitcase which is already packed
and off to her mothers;
As for you, you're left there, not
knowing what just took place or to
put it simpler, what just hit you;

I mean even if you manage to put in the word "sorry" or "ok", that will not help, her mind is made up and it will take you for ever to persuade her to come back, and that is travelling to her mother's house day in day out;
Of course the first few "visits" there you'll have your father in law to deal with;
He'll come out of the house telling you or rather calling you names and how dare you "treat" his little princess like that and bla-bla-bla; but, in a polite sort of way;
One thing you should be glad though, the first few visits you will not have a "close encounter" with the mother in law;
She is liable to "lynch" you;
Now here comes the "tricky" part;
If you really love your wife and of course your little one, you will be more or less consistent and every day you will be outside your in-laws house until she'll come out and talk to you;
That is the "weakness" all women have;
All this time she was locked up in

mommy's house she was really
suffering but her "ego" wouldn't
let go; In fact, everyone in that
house are in the same boat really;
Can you imagine living with one's
parents…?
Can you imagine the parents, no
matter how much they love their
daughter and grandchild, living
with them…?
So, everyone in that house is
let's say "on the receiving end"
You on the other hand respect them
and don't really want to have a
"go" at them so, patiently wait
until she decides to come out for
a chat;
Of course she wouldn't dare tell
you how much she'll want to come
home, that will be like throwing
in the white towel, oh no;
She'll pretend she's as happy
staying there and for ever if need
be or necessary;
That is, until you promise her
she'll have what she wants;
And of course you will;
I mean you don't really have a
choice in the matter, you either
have the house re-mortgaged or you
run the risk of loosing it

entirely; and I mean through divorce;
You'll do anything she wants and that is final;
So she takes her stuff and follows you home;
From now on, you are no longer "the mucho man" you once were, no longer the one who wears the pants in the house; you have indeed lost that title the minute you said "please darling come home"
From now on you are scared to say or do anything you know she does not like or approve off;
What I am trying to say here is… you should have thought of the phrase that says, "Prevention is a lot cheaper than repairs"
And trust me when I say, that phrase applies to almost anything or everything if you will;
If you, yes you, the one reading this, if you are indeed not married yet, maybe it is a good thing to remember that phrase; maybe even make sure you remember it, it will come in handy one day;
As for the rest of you, well, all I can say is commiserations;
So, the next thing you will do is

travel to your bank to arrange a
loan or re-mortgage your house;
Ha, the minute you will start
filling in the form, your mind
will play a little game with you;
I am almost sure the first thing
that will come to your mind is…
why…?
I mean your wife is a decent
woman, she loves you, she loves
the baby, and everything appears
to be in order; why would she
insist of having a plastic
surgery…?
I mean who "else" is going to see
what's underneath her clothes…?
That is the time you will cry out
and a little bit loud even;
"Holly shit"
Is she having an affair… and if
she is, with whom…?
Hahaha, with whom… as if it makes
any difference;
For a minute or so you will stop
filling in the blanks and think;
"If she really is having an
affair, why do I have to pay for
having it done"?
"Why isn't that bastard paying for
it, whoever he is"?
That form will be there in front

of you and you will be in two
minds whether to continue or not
or rather couldn't even if you
wanted to, just by thinking that
way;
I assure you one thing, if all
that goes through your mind you
will not fill it; period;
Of course you will ask your self
there and then one thing and one
thing alone;
"What the hell do I do now"?
Oh a million things will go
through your brains;
Your mind will work on double
quick time;
I mean, can one imagine being in
that sort of situation…?

So You Think You Know It All Huh...?
(Life's "Short" Journey)
Chapter Ten

Well, one thing for sure;
You will now do "the detective"
You will find an excuse with the bank and run out of there;
By now your mind is pre-occupied on one thing and one thing alone;
Find out if all what went through your mind is true;
You will be somewhat convinced of her being guilty, but can't prove anything yet;
The first thing you will do is change your "timing"
Find excuses to leave work earlier so you'll surprise your wife by coming home early;
You will be late going to work because you'll be hiding somewhere waiting for her to come out of the house and follow her;
This is where I simply must remind you that women in general are more cleaver than we give them credit

for and yes, more cleaver than men; whether we accept that fact or not or at least if that will make you feel a little better, the one's that are indeed having a secret affair;
These ones are the ones that have what I call "the sixth sense"
They know what they do is wrong and if they don't want to get caught they make sure they don't;
No matter how many times you'll ask the same question every morning, "What will you do today" the answer is always the same;
"Oh I'll visit my school mate…"
And if she is indeed "guilty" she'll come up with more of the same and many times you'll be hearing the…
"I'll go to moms"
And she'll be telling the truth, oh yes, she will go there, the point is, probably for half an hour or so, just in case you followed her there;
She'll know, if you did, well, she's got her self covered;
I mean how long are you going to wait out there anyway, you'll have to go to work remember?

As I said, the "sixth sense" they
have is incredible; they'll know
when to make their move;
The next thing you know, well, you
don't really, is she's in the arms
of probably a school sweetheart;
Or even worse if she enjoys sex;
If after a few days you do not
succeed in catching her "playing
around" then you will turn to a
real detective;
Needless to mention even of how
much will that set you back;
Of course if the detective comes
up with the "goods"…?
Hahaha;
You don't really want me to tell
you what next;
That will spell "major disaster"
the ONLY thing you will gain is
the divorce papers and the bills,
everything else she takes;
Kiss the house goodbye… kiss
everything you worked all your
life for, goodbye;
You will end up in a cheap hotel
room 6x4 for a long-long time;
As for your kid, you'll be lucky
if after going to the courts time
and time and yes time again to get
some kind of visiting rights or

whatever else they call it, and that is two to three hours every other week or something close to that;
Even though it is almost "a certain" that this is the way it will end up, but for the sake or argument as I always say, you are indeed one of "the lucky" ones;
She is indeed a devoted housewife and a mother;
Now that changes things a little;
Once that thought passes through your mind that "maybe" will always be there…
Even though she is "A OK" with you, you will always be "on the alert", you know, just in case and all the rest;
And as for the money you've spent on the detective was indeed a waste of money, at least you will go to work and sleep at nights let's say "more at ease"
And to make sure your wife "get's enough" you will double your "efforts" to keep her happy, for a while at least, even though you are indeed putting in a lot of effort and use a lot of energy; after all, you are the provider

and you are still working ever so
hard to pay off all those depts.
So, you do your travelling every
day to and from work and life goes
on, and before your child becomes
nine or ten, comes yet another big
blow;
Remember that women like to
announce things in the mornings…?
One beautiful morning you come
down to the kitchen for breakfast
and bam;
She comes up with…
"I want another child"
I mean with everything that's
happened or to put it in a
different way, after the "ordeal"
you went through, and now this…
well, what can I say apart from
commiserations;
Remember who is wearing the pants
at home…?
Remember what happened last time
you disapproved…?
Remember you nearly ended up
living in a hotel…?
Remember you nearly lost
everything…?
Oh yes, all those things will
"flash" not only through your
brains but you'll "visualize"

everything too;
Trust me, you will;
And in remembering all that, you'll be so stressed out; you will not know what hit you; and that stress will not go as quick as it appeared;
You will carry that stress for a few days until you accept the fact that you and whatever you say or do, do not count, not any more;
From the day you "gave in" to the Mrs. Your life belongs to her period;

So You Think You Know It All Huh...?
(Life's "Short" Journey)
Chapter Eleven

So, what one does in situations like this, I hear you ask...?
Well, under the circumstances... my advice would be to think and rethink
again before answering;
Remember one thing; your entire life depends on what you say;
Your marriage, house, even though it still technically belongs to the bank, everything you worked for... your child;
But I'm sure that you'll give in and say yes, only because you've seen and felt what she's capable off;
Even though you'll try and think of ways not to... have another child, at the end of the day you'll find that it is a loosing battle, because, what will run through your mind will more or less drive you on the "panicky"

side of things;
You will come to a stage that you will try harder and harder if you know what I mean to have that baby, and the reason for changing your mind will be one thing and one thing alone; and that reason is… you do NOT want someone else to "father" your child, or maybe I said that the wrong way; YOU do NOT want to father someone else's child;
In other words, if you cannot provide what she wants she'll simply try "someone" else and trust me when I tell you, now days is not only easy to do but no one will blame her for that either;
Having all that in mind, you will behave like a maniac in bed, the idea alone will "bring out the beast from inside of you or to put it in a nicer way, you will "perform" like a "superman"
And of course, it won't be long before she comes up and announces the "good news"
And that will be the best news you've ever heard in a long time; Oh yes, you will be proud for your self there;

But the best part about this news
is that from now on you'll have a
good excuse to take it "easy" at
nights… rest is long overdue;
But, even though you'll be
delighted with all that, there's
also bad news really that go with
the good news;
This particulate news no one cares
or even wants to talk about;
Even though you know that,
bringing another child into this
world will cost you and I don't
mean only in money, I mean all
those other things you've been
through with bringing up the first
one and all those things you had
to give up in order to provide
more and more and all those other
things, little things that you
were thinking of having the
pleasure of enjoying at this stage
of your life; all that is now
gone;
And let's not forget the way
you've treated your wife with her
first pregnancy;
Oh I assure you, she'll want the
same treatment, if not better;
After all, she's not as young
anymore and everything should be

more or less perfect for her;
This time the maid is not going to be present from the last month of her pregnancy, oh no, this time you'll have to arrange to be there with her from the third or maximum the forth month;
As for the "costs"… hell, she wouldn't give a toss; that will be entirely your problem;
And that will mean paying a visit yet again to your friend the bank manager;
Oh he'll be happy to see you and that's for sure;
After all, you're probably paying his wages;
He'll be glad to "re-re-mortgage" your already "re-mortgaged" house
Only this time is somewhat different;
You borrowed and borrowed…?
You are still paying for "the borrowing" still as well as the "regular" mortgage payments, now you'll be paying for the first two, and because you're not able to add to those payments the bank will not say to you…
"Oh no problem, you pay whenever is convenient"

The bank will find other ways to "lynch" you, and that is the way it operates, dead slow… never in a hurry… but they always come out laughing at the end as people in general put it;
Personally I disagree with that theory;
In my opinion, banks are laughing from the minute you decide to go to them, the minute you walk through those doors, the minute your turn comes and they say to you… "Hello, how may I help you"?
In my opinion they should change that sentence to…
"Hello "victim" how may I lynch you"?
Because that is what you become from the minute you walk through those doors;
And to make things even worse, "we" practically "beg" them for a loan, as if they'll "donate" that money we need as a charitable act;
And to make matters that much more "interesting" we call our selves "intelligent" Hahaha, isn't that a joke huh…?
I mean intelligent…?
Come on…!

For example we buy a house worth 100K, we work our ass's of to pay back all that money and I mean for twenty-twenty five or maybe even thirty years and by that time the house is worth let's say 300K;
The first thing we'll think is that we made a profit… great…!!! Hahaha, think again;
If one works out the bank charges, the "hidden extras", the interest, the letters they send you and whatever else they can add "numbers" on, you'll probably end up with well over the 300K your house is worth NOW;
But if someone asks us "how much did the house cost you" you'll say 100K, never 300 plus;
But the worse part of all is if and when one decides to sell his property; aha… now there's a laugh;
You'll think you could retire on that yes…?
Well, think again; you seem to have forgotten your friend;
Oh yes, you do have a friend, one that never forgets you, he always remembers you, year in year out; you maybe, have never seen him,

but he considers you as a good if
not the best friend;
And his name is... "The Taxman"
I assure you, if you do sell... he
will be the first to congratulate
you, he will be the first in line
to... "Collect"
In other words, you will finally
meet this guy;
He will no longer be invincible;
And he will be ever so glad to
meet you at long last and I mean
in person, after all, he knows
more about you than you do;
And guess what...?
He'll come up with the phrase...
"Capital gains tax"
By the time you pay him off,
you'll find that the "life time"
you spent paying off your mortgage
and the taxman, your house is
worth "shit" really;
And don't even think you can avoid
any of the above; even if you
decide to keep the house until the
day you die;
The taxman will get his money one
way or another;
He'll change the phrase from
"capital gains to inheritance tax"
Oh he'll get his money alright and

there's nothing you can do to
change that;
So, the minute you walk through
those doors yet again they'll be
delighted to see you;
What makes me laugh is, you get
your loan and pay back your
prearranged
amount month in month
out; but there comes a time in
everyone's life that the
unexpected happens, something
unforeseen, something untoward, a
setback and of course you miss a
payment or two; Hahaha, then
you'll see your "friendly bank
managers true colors come out;
Oh they'll send you reminders and
reminders first, and don't think
that they're just letters, oh no,
every letter the bank sends, they
charge you an astronomical sum and
that sum will be added or rather
charged to your account;
Now this is what I call a "cleaver
trick"
Although they show you long faces
and all the rest, deep down, this
is what every bank in the world
hopes for, missing a few payments;
That is the time they really "love

you", they'll "pounce" on the
opportunity to charge and charge
and yes charge you with everything
they can think of;
They'll hit you so hard you
wouldn't know which end in which;
To put it a little simpler, you
miss a couple of payments; you'll
end up adding four or five more at
the end of the day;
Huh… try missing five or six
payments;
God forbid… if that happens,
they'll "hit" you with everything
they can possibly think of;
And that means, you'll add or
rather extend your
payments three or four and maybe
even five years on your original
agreement;
Simply because they'll add to
their charging you lawyer's fees,
and we all know what they charge,
they don't mess about, they don't
charge you by letter they send,
they charge for every word that's
written in that letter;
Of course you know all this or at
least you think you know but don't
want to even think about all that,
you carry on as if nothing is

wrong, only because circumstances are such, you cannot avoid any of all that;
Or maybe even you know beforehand that… if you do "fight it" and I mean the system, it is after all a lost cause;
And even if you do, or rather you're either brave enough or inexperienced, I assure you, you will end up paying and paying and I mean there's no end to it;
In other words, you belong to them now;
Commonly know as…
"They've got you by the balls"

So You Think You Know It All Huh...? (Life's "Short" Journey) Chapter Twelve

So you go ahead anyway and re-re-re-mortgage your home;
Ha... "Your" home...?
Isn't that a joke...!!!
Why don't they call it "your life"
I'll never know;
I mean let's face it or look at it the realistic way, isn't it your life you're signing away at the bank...?
And what's more don't you reconfirm
that every time you "re"
sign...?
And yes, there's another thing that I disapprove of in this world;
"The small print"
I mean halloo... small print...?
123
And it is not only the banks; nearly everything in this world has a small print somewhere;

I mean they make sure it is
printed so small, even with a
magnifying glass is hard to read;
And to make things even worse,
they use some kind of language
that even they don't understand
half of what it says;
They come up with words that even
in dictionaries do not exist;
Why…?
I mean isn't that a "clear"
indication that they're trying to
"trick you" into something…?
What I want to know is what and
mainly when are governments around
the world are "finally" going to
do something and why haven't they
done anything yet about this…?
I thought "fraud" was against the
law and the same law is enforced
in every country in the world, and
yet, these people are allowed to
trick you, to me these "tricky"
businesses sounds like they
approve of the entire thing or the
entire system if you like;
In fact, I am convinced of that;
The entire thing is more like a
chain reaction and at the very end
of that chain is indeed
governments and I explain;

If there's a mishap or a cock-up or something, the first thing you'll know is you'll end up in court, and be sure that you'll be found guilty of whatever the charges may be, only because you haven't read the "small print" in the first place before signing;
And that means you'll end up paying a fortune to… first the lawyer's and second the courts; and yes, I said courts and the reason for that is simple, "they" the legal system are in agreement in my opinion, they'll "postpone" the proceedings for a few times so as they'll charge you more and more; and if you think that lawyers charge a fortune, hahaha, wait till you see how much the courts charge;
And if by any chance you find some kind of courage to protest against the decision, well, you'll end up paying a heavy fine on top or even find your self behind bars;
And yet, we like to say "we live in a free world"
Freedom of speech, freedom of expressions, free to do this and free to do that;

But only when we attempt to "use" some of those so called "freedoms" we actually realize that we might as well be in chains;
Hahaha… freedom my ass…
To me this is what I call "foul play"
To me it is simply "bullshit"
It is all approved by the legal system to earn more and more;
Maybe, some of you guys out there are somewhat upset (to say the least) from the way I express my "anger" and use "foul" lingo etc… but, this is me, I am being honest here and I do hope you will appreciate that;
Now I don't know about you lot out there if or what you're going to do about all this, but I found a way to put forward my protest against all this "foul play" and that is the only way I know how "In black and white"
After all, it is the only way I can reach everyone;
Well, at least I am doing something however little it may sound;
The question is what will you do about it…?

Yes you, the one who's reading this; Halloo… what…???
Don't just sit there feeling sorry for your self either, you are and always will be another "victim";
Now days there's the internet… so…?
Use it man… call everyone you know and in turn they'll do the same and before you know it… well, do you really want me to carry on…???
From now on it is all up to you guys;
I am indeed too old for such "excitements"
So, back to our story; as I was saying, you go ahead and get the loan and that means one thing and one thing alone;
You're back to where you started; and that is, the beginning of your married life, only difference is you are older by a few years and more the wiser, or so you think and of course this time around with a family of your own that need your support, and I don't mean only financially, but physically and mentally too;
Of course you don't want to let them down do you…?

So you go through all that all
over again and I mean the months
of your wife's pregnancy and all
that she needs… getting a maid in…
And of course this time around you
have another kid that needs-needs
need;
You have to find a way not only to
pay for everything but keep
everyone happy too;
As for your self or your needs…
forget it, they simply don't count
or more appropriate, you are not
allowed to even think of things
like that;
From now on it's not only
providing money for everything but
you are expected to provide
physical and mental help too;
And all that on a 24/7 basis;
From now on, no one will judge you
by how hard you work but how and
what you provide at home;
And as time passes you go through
all that you've been through with
your first child;
And lady luck for once is on your
side; oh yes, we must not forget
lady luck do we, and one day your
boss comes to your office to
announce to you personally the

good news;
"Congratulations, you are promoted to… and you're getting a raise"
Suddenly, just when you least expected it, things are starting to look up;
I mean let's face it; the law of averages applies to everything and everyone, yes, even to you;
Surely "luck" will come your way sooner or later;
Of course your boss is too proud to say "you deserved it", hell no; he'll come and say for example "to fill in the position of the retired colleague and what's more, I expect from you… and bla-bla"
In other words not that you so richly deserve it and all that but you'll be there on a trial basis;
Of course he will congratulate you and usually before leaving he'll come up with these words…
"I hope you won't let me down"
But you and the entire world know that, he really wants to say…
"Make sure you earn what you get"
Of course you know that for every penny you get, you, more or less have to produce ten for him and there's nothing you could do to

alter that because, you always have that little phrase at the back of your mind reminding you of something, and that phrase goes like this;
"If you cannot… I'll find someone who can"
Having that in mind, you simply put your tail between your legs and just say thank you "boss"
In other words, you are indeed so scared in case he changes his mind and offer the position to someone else; you are indeed liable to even kiss his ass for that position;
Even though you think about it constantly, you'll be a little upset, but that will not last long, the raise you'll get will be enough to put all that behind you;
And until the day your boss will come and say "yes, I am satisfied with your performance" or something along those lines, you will keep that promotion news a secret… just in case;
Oh I know, some of you lot out there would love to say to your miserable boss where to go or where to stuff the job…

But, if there are people who
depend on you and bla-bla-bla, you
simply cannot and will not do or
say anything else except theses
two words
"Thank you"
In other words;
Because of your "status" your boss
simply has you at a position you
cannot do anything else;
Yet again;
He's got you by the balls;

So You Think You Know It All Huh...?
(Life's "Short" Journey)
Chapter Thirteen

But for arguments sake (as I always say) everything turns out fine and yes, the promotion is indeed there to stay or rather yours to keep, extra money comes in, and you can afford to say more often "yes" without having to "sweat" for it; life in other words is finally smiling at you, or rather for you for a change;
All that will have an effect on you; well, at least it will put a smile in your face, and that smile was long-long overdue;
But, due to past experiences, and being more the wiser, you will keep that news to your self for as long as possible, well, until you come to a stage that the bank manager will see you with a smile in his face;
But don't let that fool you, that smile is a "pretence" one, he or

she was trained for that and
trained really well; all that
pretence is to lure you in and
borrow-borrow if and when you're
in need again;
That "smile" will be enough to
"temp" you to… "Rush" to them the
minute you find yourself in a bit
of trouble;
And let me assure you of one
thing;
Getting in to trouble financially
is as easy as ABC… especially
after promotion and the raise in
salary;
If one is not careful enough and
leaves all that go through his/her
head, and I mean thinking that you
could afford everything now and
bla-bla-bla;
And of course… before you know it
you are a father of two;
Although by now you know what to
expect and of course what's
expected of you, you think life
will be that much easier;
Ha… think again, now the "demand"
is more or less twice as big;
The effort you'll need to "put in"
is far greater than you think;
Now you have a new born, but you

also have another kid around who
is growing at an alarming rate and
his demands are indeed greater and
greater each and every day;
You have to take him to school
every day, bring him back, help
him with his homework, take him
out for some fresh air, feed him
if required, put him to bed;
But at the same time your wife
will want as much help as possible
too you know;
Get me this, bring me that, go
shopping, don't forget to get this
and don't forget to bring that;
As for night time…?
Well, I think by now you know what
to expect, the baby screaming and
keeping you awake… and all that
you suffered with your first born;
The baby illnesses and what to do…
the doctors visits… and all the
rest of the every day little
things;
Ha… little they may be but, they
take a lot of time and effort from
you to… let's say put right;
I mean I could go into details of
every day life at that stage but I
think you got the picture;
And the same routine will be on

and on for a few years until your little one starts going to kindergarten or play school if you like;
By that time of course you will have a kid in play school but also a kid who by now is a teenager and in high school;
And being in high school or at that age we all know how vulnerable he could be;
He will need you now more than ever before and that means spending time with him;
At this stage, one can only hope that the kid will not be tempted to try drugs, as drugs are indeed the teenagers way of entertaining now days;
Drugs are in my opinion THE disease of the twenty first century; but I also believe that we, the parents are to blame for that; and when I say we, I mean the parents;
Most of the parents have them selves to blame if their kid turns to drugs; I think most of the kids who try or turn to drugs are the one's who are bored, the one's who have everything they ever wished

for and there's nothing else to do, so why not try that too huh…?
I just hope that some parents out there take note of what I said, and maybe, just maybe I am indeed right in what I said and if with what I said will "save" even one kid out there from all that, that for me is a "victory" if I was permitted to use that word;
I know some of you parents out there would say… it's easy for you to say, but I want my kid to have everything I never had and bla-bla-bla;
Yes I agree with you but up to a point;
In my opinion though, too much of everything is why the kids of today are drugs because that is the only thing left… they have everything else…
I wonder if there's someone out there who disagrees with me;
It would be interesting to here opinions on this matter;
But however big the importance of this and opinions and even arguments on this could go on and on the fact of the matter is indeed another story altogether

So You Think You Know It All Huh...?
(Life's "Short" Journey)
Chapter Fourteen

So, the same routine will go on and on... until your big boy graduates from high school and is in two minds whether to go collage or not;
This is the time, you as the "head" of the family, will do your "magic" and persuade the kid and that is for his own good and bla-bla-bla... even though you know that it will cost you an arm and a leg;
But what can one do really; it's one of those things;
After all, it is your duty as a father to provide, at least education for your offspring;
Don't forget, they didn't ask to come to this world;
I mean whether one can afford this or not, one should find a way...
And this is what I was saying a wile back, remember...?
Why is it that people should pay

and yes, a fortune, if I may add, for educating one's own children…? Is it really only for the kid…? I really wonder… What kind of government will be, or better still, what sort of a country will one have to live in without educated people…?
I know I keep going back to the same subject and some of you out there mite get or rather find this a little… shall we say boring, but for those who find them selves in that position will indeed understand a little bit more, and why I say that…?
Because now days… when a subject does not affect us directly, we, humans, tend to ignore it, as if to say… who cares, let the ones concerned deal with it;
Unfortunately, this is what humans became, we only see what is profitable or the "near future" and worse even, if it's profitable "enough" and I mean here and now, not tomorrow or the day after;
We became so greedy and selfish; we simply do not give a shit about no one or anything any more, unless of course there's something

to gain;
I was brought up to respect people
and volunteer if help was needed;
Now days that is a thing of the
past, or worse even, now days if
one volunteers for something he or
she would be named "suckers"
Some people they'll even say… (If
one volunteers to help)
"You had nothing else to do
anyway… so, consider this as… a
receiving favor"
What is the world coming to…?
But… yes, you guess it, that is
indeed another story;

So You Think You Know It All Huh...?
(Life's "Short" Journey)
Chapter Fifteen

So, as I was saying, routine life, day in day out... going to work... taking the kids to school... going shopping... look after the family... managing to keep up with the mortgage...
Good days and bad days, sad days and exciting days;
Good days are the ones that you hear no bad news;
Sad days are the ones you turn the telly on for the news, but all you hear is bad news;
Sad days are the ones you hear of a friend or relative has died;
And this routine life will go on until you reach your fifties;
That is the time where you'll start feeling a little different every day that passes;
That is the time where, some people say...
"The beginning of the end"

Some others say…
"Now it is downhill all the way"
That is the time where you will
hear all that from everyone out
there if the subject comes up;
And even though you feel you are
still young-ish, in hearing all
that, one tends to "suffer" if
that is the right word
psychological;
All that talk and phrases and I
don't know what else… will make
you think and think deep;
"Is it really my turn"…?
"Has my time come up"…?
"I wonder how long more I can hang
on"…?
"Will I still be around to see my
children married"…?
"Will I have enough time left to
play with my grandchildren"…?
"Will I have another twenty good
years to go without illnesses"…?
"How quick the fifty years went"…?
And those five or six questions
are just a small example of what
will go through your mind, and I
do mean day in day out;
I mean if one is "not there yet"
to know first hand, one could only
imagine really;

So imagine, being in your fifties…
having a wife and two almost grown
up kids… mortgage still on for at
least ten years more… one of your
kids is in university and the
other in collage… expenses are
running at an alarming rate… wages
are at a standstill… and the idea
of… the best years of your life
are indeed long gone… well, what
can I say apart from good luck and
hope you do have at least twenty
"good years" left;
I will go as far as to mention
something about jobs too;
I mean now days, no one is really
sure of anything any more;
No one can say "I have a secure
job" any more;
With this "modern" system if one
comes to a stage where his wages
are a little higher than everyone
else, they simply give you the
sack, well, now days even the word
"sack" is modernized; the new
version of "sack" now is
"redundant"
They'll give you something of
course just to shut you up and…
bye-bye;
You see, nothing and no one is

irreplaceable any more; and
especially with all these factors...
Globalization and robots;
I mean there are arguments and
arguments about this; every one in
this world has his or her opinion;
My argument, my version, my way of
thinking, my way of whatever one
cares to name it is...
Some greedy bastards out there
took the word or idea of
"capitalism" and they abused it;
and in doing so, they abuse the
ordinary poor guy, and that means
families and families;
I mean is that a joke or is it a
joke;
Lately all one listens from the
news is... this firm or rather this
guy... placed a takeover bid for
that firm for so many billions...!!!
I mean I ask you, what is this guy
trying to do... make money...???
I mean, taking his point of view,
I don't really blame him; he is
trying ever so hard to avoid the
taxman; (the capitalism system)
Now one could see what I mean when
I said "abuse"
I am not saying that capitalism is
necessarily a bad thing, oh no, it

has its good parts too; what I am trying to say is why not put a limit somewhere; can't "the system" change a little…?
If this is to carry on and on… how will the "little" guy survive…?
I think, governments should introduce a "bill" saying;
If you can afford all that money and I mean "zillions" to buy this that and the other… you should pay so much in taxes AND abolish the taxes on the workers;
Now I do not know or care for that matter, what that idea comes under, whether it is capitalism or socialism or even communism, or maybe some other "thing" that I know nothing about either; all I know it is the only way the "little" or the ordinary family will survive;
But I also know that… who would listen to "Little and humble old me" huh…?
But… yet again, that is another story;
Let's go back to the original;
As I was saying, you have managed to reach your fifties, "bravo"
Yes, you do deserve that praise;

Now days (in my opinion) that is indeed an achievement; especially when having to raise a family and all that that goes with it, a full mortgage and of course still in one piece; well, a simple bravo is indeed too little to say the least;
From now on, every time you look into the mirror you will notice that you are getting "greyer and greyer"
From now on you will start counting your grey hairs at first and slowly but surely that will turn around, meaning you will start counting your original color hair and how many are left;
That is indeed the "confirmation" if you will of "the downhill" and the worse part of it all is… you started this downhill with no brakes at all;
Ha… needles to explain what that means;
The good thing about that age is that you do not feel old… yet;
Even though one could say you had a hard-ish life and you should, the fact remains, you don't;
You feel as if you still can go on

and on;
It is only on your birthdays that
from now on you will feel sad
really, only because you are
indeed mature enough to understand
that, yet another year is gone and
there aren't that many left;
Once your kids graduate and
they're established or have a
descent job, all you have to look
forward to is for them to get
married and of course
grandchildren;
Oh you will love your
grandchildren twice as much I
assure you;
Grandparents around the world
confirm that;
Some even say… they are "twice"
your own;
Oh the joy they will give you…!!!
And when they're around, you will
feel as if you are the luckiest
person on earth;
That is if your kids listen to you
or respect your opinion as a
father and as an older man;
If on the other hand one or even
both your kids "ignore" a few of
your advices… well what can I say;

Hat I am trying to say here is, If
you are for example a little
prejudiced and you happen to...
let's say "dislike" a race or
color or something along those
lines; well... I am sorry to inform
you that nine out of ten times,
kids go against your "believes"
And what will be the "killer blow"
for you is if one of your kids is
a girl;
Killer blow my be called yes, but
I assure you it no way near "a
blow" but a constant torture every
single day of your life;
After all, your daughter will
bring home this guy that you
despise and you will either see
him every day or maybe every so
often; and that fact you would
have wished it was indeed just one
killer blow and that is it, you're
gone; but no way, I assure you if
you happen to be the guy with such
a problem, then is sure death, but
a slow one, and I do mean "slow"
Even though you will try and try
to get it out of your mind, you
will find that, that is
impossible; and you will not

believe the effect it will have on you;
The damage in someone's guts this "thing" does is beyond repairs and that I assure you of;
You will find your self visiting your doctor more often than you want to from now on;
Hell; if you are indeed one of "unlucky" fathers, the pills and pills you will consume, medicine after medicine; and that could turn even worse for you because we all know all medicines have side effects;
You will go to bed every night and the only thing in your mind will be "I failed as a father"
But for the sake of argument, let's say you are not "one of those"

So You Think You Know It All Huh…? (Life's "Short" Journey) Chapter Sixteen

But time flies, and there's no stopping it or even slowing it down a bit, and before you realize it, you're in your sixties;
Aha… that magic number;
Now is the time that you really, not only look foreword to your retirement but plan it in such a way as to have "it" as easy as possible;
But things do not work out as we want them, do they…?
No matter how much you tried to save up for that, there's always something to spend it on;
Whether that is some unexpected illness or the house is in need of repairs, or maybe even the grandson is in need and for some reason you could not refuse;
Even at work things are from now on just not the same;
You will find that every one of

your colleagues is treating you
somewhat different; they more or
less give you less to do;
As if they're telling you (in a
silent way) you are finished;
And that is were you will feel the
"oldness" in you;
And until the day you actually
retire, that feeling will be
stronger and stronger;
Especially your last year;
Oh that is the "killer blow"
You will feel so bad going there
every day knowing that they all
want you out ASAP and they cannot
wait to see that day;
And why, I hear you ask…?
Simple;
Every one of them is after your
position;
And to impress the boss, they'll
work harder… even work overtime
without any extra benefits;
All that you will witness and
probably laugh about it;
And the last two or three months
at work, you will see that there
will be no work for you to do at
all, your boss will share your
"load" to everyone else there, he
will even ask you to take days and

days off if not retire completely
the last two or three months and
yes with full wages;
Oh yes, "cleaver" bosses now days
do that sort of thing;
I mean let's face it, he want to
vacate you position as soon as
possible, so a younger person will
take your place, they always have
this idea that being young they
work harder;
Or maybe you will be asked to
train someone, your replacement;
As far as he is concerned "The
show must go on"

So You Think You Know It All Huh...?
(Life's "Short" Journey)
Chapter Seventeen

Even though you'll come to the stage where you will hate your self going to work these last couple of months, and of course look forward to the big day that you'll shake hands with everyone and say your goodbyes, that day will come and sooner than you think;

Of course when the final day is indeed here, there will be a small party sort of speak, maybe half an hour or so, just enough for you and your boss to say a few words cut the cake and have a drink, receive from everyone a hand shake and well wishes;

The good thing about this retirement business is that you get a "fat-ish" check for your services all these years, and trust me when I tell you; even though it is a Fat check, it is

enough only to pay off the bank for your house;
All you'll have now is your pension money to look forward to every month and that is it;
That is all well and good and maybe even the first few days you will say thank God for that;
But you wait till you get your official papers and your first "retirement check"
I assure you of one thing;
Instead of being happy for getting some money and all that… something else will happen;
It will suddenly "hit" you straight in the brains;
The first thing you will think is… that is it; you are finished and that is official;
I mean that cheque is the "final" thing you are involved in;
That cheque is a reminder that… there's nothing else left for you in this life except death;
I mean let's face it, is there anything else to look forward to…?
That fact will send you into a deep depression, and I do mean deep;
You will lock your self to your

self for a few days and even weeks
until you get the next pension
cheque and that is the time you'll
be more let's say at ease…
But that first month, I tell you,
you will be so stressed out, so
depressed so un-talkative, it will
be the worse month of your life;
But, bear in mind that even your
so called beloved country, the
country you've offered so much
over the years, is now considering
you as a "pest"
What I am trying to say is… you do
not contribute any more do you…?
So, do you really believe that
your so called government is happy
to send you money every month…?
Oh they might say yes, we love our
pensioners and we'll do this for
them and that for them, but all
that is just a show from their
part just to get your vote or
rather convince you to vote for
them;
The minute they're elected and "up
there" you mean nothing to them,
in fact they hate your guts for
"being around still"
Don't be fooled from what they say
and promise, that is all a real

live show and nothing else;
To me, all that is plain bullshit,
they'll say and promise anything
so long as they sit on that
"throne"
For me, all politicians are the
same or one of a kind with
lawyers, "Born liars" and nothing
or anyone in this world could
convince me otherwise;
Oh I know I keep getting away from
my story but, can you blame me...?
But as I keep saying... that is
another story;

So You Think You Know It All Huh...?
(Life's "Short" Journey)
Chapter Eighteen

But as I said, that second and maybe the third cheque will put you at ease, it will indeed make you feel somewhat better;
Only because you haven't after all "kicked the bucket" yet, and life does indeed exist or goes on, even after retirement age;
But there's yet another setback for you at this age;
Every day that passes, you are indeed getting older and older, and no one comes to see you any more, even your own children or grandchildren are either too busy to pay you a visit, or they'll come up with some excuse to avoid you, and why...?
Simple, you are indeed too old for them, nothing to discuss, no advice you can offer that they do not already know;
Even if your wife is still around,

you'll have nothing to talk about
any more, not after all these
years together;
So what's left…?
Well, you are simply left there in
a world of your own; a world of
reminiscing and of course talking
to your self;
Assuming you are healthy still,
you go for short walks in the near
by park, sit on every one of those
benches for a breather and back to
the house;
That is your life from now on;
Oh every so often you will get a
visit from your sons and
grandkids; and that will please
you enormously; but these visits
are few and far between and they
have a purpose;
They do not visit you because they
love, oh no, they are just
checking if you're fit enough to
live in the house alone or
persuade you to move into a
retirement home, just for you to
get out of the house;
The truth of the matter is, they
are indeed waiting for you to…
kick the bucket, just to sell the
house and get the money;

Of course when at that age one feels all this and try to "hang on" as much as possible;
But the truth of the matter is… time is not on your side any more and every day that passes is another day closer to the inevitable; either you'll kick the bucket or come to a stage where you cannot cope by your self any more and that mean straight into one of these "homes"
Oh yes; they'll dump in there alright, none of your kids would want you to stay with them and usually the excuse is… "My wife does not want" or more common… We do not have the room"
The truth of the matter is, as I said before, you being around still is… to put it mildly, "A killer" for them, as far as they are concerned, being still "here" at your age is unacceptable, and the only thing on their minds or rather in their brains is… "What is the point of living still at this age"
I mean if you really think about it, they do have a point;
But life is so sweet as some

people call it and all living
things try to hang on as much as
possible;
But as I said before, I disagree
with that theory;
I believe people try desperately
to hang on because of fear; fear
of the unknown; People simply do
not know what is after death and
they fear in case it is worse than
what they know or been through;
And that, more or less sums up the
average middle class "westerner's"
life;
Of course there are exceptions and
exceptions, some better and some
worse off; some lucky in life and
some not so lucky; some are born
into poverty and some into
richness;
But, as I usually say;
"That is another story"
And that's it really;
From now on, one can only "wait"
for the inevitable, and we all
know what that is;
I mean at that age, what else is
there to wait for…???
Well, one could argue that point I
suppose, only for the fact that no
one knows when exactly is time,

but even so, when one goes past
the age of let's say eighty, what
else is there to expect…?
What I cannot comment about at
that age (as I am not "there"
yet)is… do people actually "give
up" do they look forward to…
whatever is let's say waiting for
them…?
Or maybe they just give up because
of all that hardship life they had
and just want to "rest"
Whatever the case may be or rather
whatever the reason, one thing and
I do mean only one thing is for
sure; and that is THE END IS NEAR;
Or to put it in a different way,
THE END IS CLOSE and sometimes
closer than we know or hope for;
It only remains for me to thank
you for buying this book and for
sharing my thoughts and ideas;
Of course I could have gone into
more detail, or analyze or maybe
describe in detail of "our"
everyday life, but that would have
taken me a lifetime to write it
all down and you, ha… a lifetime
to read it all;

Thank you again and allow me to "remind" you of one important thing to remember;

"Life is indeed a wonderful "Gift" no matter how good or hard it turns out to be;

We (humans) always try to better it, there's no doubt about that, the point is how do we go about it...?

If only people realize that the best way or maybe the "only" way to do that is simply... appreciate life that little bit more; and although life is indeed a gift to us, and yes, we do think it's ours to do whatever we please with it; but surely a big question arises here;

"Is it really "ours" to keep"...???
God Bless you all

Antonio Salacuri

www.ingramcontent.com/pod-product-compliance
Ingram Content Group UK Ltd.
Pitfield, Milton Keynes, MK11 3LW, UK
UKHW041437180426
11947UKWH00007B/484